LEAD LIKE YOU MEAN IT!

6 Steps to Building a Team that People Want to Be a Part of!

LORI A. STRODE

Lead Like You Mean It!
Lori A. Strode

Copyright © 2013 by Lori A. Strode

Published By:
Northern Azimuth Coaching, LLC
1121 Elisabeth Dr. O'Fallon, IL 62269, USA
info@northernazimuthcoaching.com
http://www.northernazimuthcoaching.com

ISBN 13: 978-0-9894999-5-8

Published in the United States of America

Book Design by www.KarrieRoss.com

DEDICATION

This book is dedicated to the Soldiers, Sailors, Airmen, and Marines who have dedicated their lives to preserving the freedom of our country. Thank you for your service!

Lori A. Steele

ABOUT THE AUTHOR

Lori has been a leader for over 22 years as she has trained, mentored, coached, and developed Soldiers and Officers in the <u>Army National Guard</u>, the <u>United States Army,</u> and other branches of our Armed Services.

In addition to her career in the military Lori has been a teacher and counselor to over 2,400 at-risk youth, the Director of Admissions and Graduate Affairs for one of the largest Youth <u>ChalleNGe</u> programs in the United States, and the Director of Mentoring and Case Management for approximately 1,800 students and their mentors.

Lori has numerous hours of experience performing and developing leadership workshops and staff training workshops, as well as performing as a motivational speaker. She has held positions at every level of management, including the executive and strategic levels.

Lori has a Master's Degree in Human Resource Development and is a Certified Life Coach with specialty designations in Executive and Business Leadership, Health and Wellness and Personal Life Coaching. Lori is the CEO and Co-Founder of Northern Azimuth Coaching, LLC.

FOREWORD

When I received Lori's request to write the foreword for her new book, I asked myself why. Why, out of all (literally hundreds) of her contacts, colleagues, fans and friends does she want me, a retired Sergeant Major, to write a foreword to a book about leadership, motivation and team-building. Despite this, I accepted enthusiastically for two reasons; Lori and her message.

It didn't take me long to figure out her reasoning. After all, I was her hardest nut to crack. I wasn't as crusty as Sam Elliot's character in *We Were Soldiers* but I was just as unapproachable. I believed work was work and I kept my personal life private and out of the way. There was no room in the workplace for fun, laughter, or relationships. This was the Army; there were standards, one way of training and nothing warm, fuzzy or entertaining about it. For someone who had all the answers, I knew nothing.

What you have in your hands is 22 years of leadership wisdom unlike you have ever experienced before. Like Lori, this book is fresh, funny and incredibly insightful. It reads as if you are sitting and having a conversation with the author. She freely shares life lessons, family anecdotes, personal beliefs, successes and failures. Its roots lay in common sense, people smarts and tested truths.

Regardless of who you are, what you do, where you're going or why you picked up this book, there is something here for everyone. Neatly packaged in six simple steps, Lori outlines and explains what you need to do in order to become a better leader, businessman/woman, partner, friend or person.

Throughout the book are examples and suggestions that clearly demonstrate every step of her *D.I.R.E.C.T* approach and why each is essential. Further, she enhances your understanding by leaving you "hints"....the intended take-away from a particular discussion.

Inspiration, motivation and enthusiasm are infectious and hard to deny even for the most impervious of personalities (Army Sergeants Major included). I have witnessed and experienced the wild successes these principles manifest. As you build your team and move toward or increase your own success stories, keep this book close. You will want to reference it over and over again. Highlight it, dog ear pages, write in its margins and share the message with others. A wise woman once told me; "Once you are a star, the next level is to make other stars." I couldn't have done it without her guidance, counsel and friendship.

Tamy J. Kuzel
Aka "Catwoman" (This will make more sense later in the book)
Sergeant Major (RET)
Springfield, Illinois 2013

ACKNOWLEDGMENTS

I have not attempted to cite in the text all of the authorities and sources consulted in the preparation of this book. To do so would require more space than is available.

Valuable information, mentoring, and inspiration were contributed by Anthony Robbins; John Eggen; Dan Poynter; Karrie Ross; Chris Lawson; Michael Haerr; Paul Hastings; Katherine Kobliner; Mark Cuttle; Dana Whaley; Marisa Bealor; Lisa Tepas; Tamy Kuzel; Earl Mashaw, Maura Workman and numerous members of the Illinois Army National Guard, specifically members and former members of the 634th Brigade Support Battalion, members of Joint Task Force Phoenix J4 section, and staff members of The Lincoln's Challenge Academy (you know who you are); My parents, Ron and Ada Strode, and my family and friends who provided constant motivation and inspiration.

I sincerely thank all of you! This book would not be possible without your inspiration, mentoring, and friendship.

WARNING—DISCLAIMER

INTRODUCTION

Over the years there has been a great deal of debate over the definition of leadership, what makes a great leader, and how to be an effective leader. Some believe that there is a specific set of characteristics or traits that a great leader must possess.

There are some schools of thought that state that there are different traits required for different career fields. Some will tell you that money provides a platform for power and eventually an appointment into a leadership position.

We certainly can't rule out the theory of born or bred, which philosophizes that a leader is either born a leader or that a person can be developed into a leader. In simple terms, the "born" philosophy doesn't believe that you can train, mentor, coach, or develop a person to become a leader; rather that you are either born a leader or you are not.

Contrary to the born theory the bred theory believes that you can teach someone to become a leader, regardless of having been born with certain characteristics or traits.

Yet another philosophy, by the late Dr. Stephen Covey, an internationally respected leadership authority and author, states that leadership is a choice not a position. This perspective implies that leadership is about attitude not title.

No matter what your philosophy, I think we can all agree that we have encountered individuals in leadership positions that were phenomenal and those that had no business anywhere near a leadership role.

In this book I'm going to share with you one approach to leadership that has served me well for over 22 years, I call it the

D.I.R.E.C.T Approach to Leadership. I fine-tuned and developed this leadership style with the help of great mentors, peers, and subordinates and just recently put it on paper as a model, technique, or approach to leadership. I have been asked, in the past, to share my approach and have done so during leadership conferences, training seminars, and forums but I have never written it into a scripted format until now.

The *D.I.R.E.C.T Approach* is simple, not fancy, not cold, as the title may imply, not calculated, and certainly not complicated. Call it an approach, a philosophy, or a model but the bottom line is when used, genuinely, it works. It's about the humanity of leadership and how small strategies and techniques make a world of difference to those being led. I challenge you to absorb, consider, evaluate, and implement this approach and see how it works for you.

Even if this is completely out of your comfort zone, at least give it a try for 30 days, and I promise you will see a difference. You will see the benefits in increased productivity in individuals as well as your entire team. You will find the return on your investment will be worth your while.

This approach has served me well over the years, and I am confident that you will find it useful, if not essential, to your success and the success of your team.

CONTENTS

CHAPTER 1

Outstanding leaders go out of their way to
boost the self-esteem of their personnel.
If people believe in themselves, it's amazing
what they can accomplish.

~ **Sam Walton**, Founder of Wal-Mart ~

回 凹

MIRROR, MIRROR ON THE WALL?

How do you know you want to be a leader? When did you
know that you wanted to be a leader? I asked myself these
questions as I began conceptualizing this book, and not
surprisingly, I couldn't define one "a-ha" moment when I determined that I was going to be a leader or even what made me
decide to strive to become one. What I determined was that it
wasn't an event that brought me to my decision, but rather my
experiences with people that ultimately developed the leader
that I am today. I would venture to guess that most of those
people didn't even realize the impact they had on me or that
they were contributing to the development of what kind of
a leader I would become. For most, it was just who they

were—ordinary people living their lives and quietly impacting the next generation of leaders.

I grew up in Gilman, Illinois, a small farming community, population 1,800. A town where everyone you passed on the street would give you the "one finger" wave as they lifted their index finger off the steering wheel when they passed to acknowledge and greet you as you drove by them. A town where farmers would gather in the local truck stop (K & H) to discuss the old days, this year's yield, or upcoming sales and auctions. Depending on the time of year, they would occupy THEIR seat for hours and drink endless cups of coffee and leave a miniscule tip for the waitresses that dutifully served them day in and day out. A town where sporting events, specifically boys' basketball and football, were religiously attended and supported by the student body, the faculty, and a large majority of the community. In fact, some of the most exciting things that happened in Gilman were the result of sporting events, at least for me. And my favorite characteristic about my small town: like most, my Mom and Dad knew what had happened at school that day before I even got home to tell them, and sometimes that wasn't a good thing.

No stop lights, one fast food restaurant, two town cops, three truck stops, four churches, a five and dime, six bars, and an entire town full of good hearted, hardworking people with an occasional scandal that swept the town like wild fire and gave the boys at the truck stop something else to talk about.

When I was a resident of that small town I was frequently bored out of my mind, as are most children and teenagers, due to the lack of things to do. The closest mall was 45 minutes away, the swimming pool, the movie theater, and even McDonalds were all in another town. No museums, no professional or collegiate sporting teams in town. No paint ball, no zip lines, and no concert halls.

As I reflect back on these memories of my youth I realize that small town, what it stood for, and the people that lived there are a large reason that I am who I am today, in spite of what my younger self thought the town was lacking. I learned pride as we rallied around our sports teams, adorning ourselves with face paint, school colors, and rally towels as we rooted for the hometown team. I learned values and respect and to never, under any circumstances, call an adult by anything other than his or her title and last name. I learned what it means to be part of a team and how a leader fits into that equation. Upon reflection, there were many large and small lessons that I learned living in my small town, even though at the time I couldn't wait to leave. Funny how life works, isn't it?

As you read through this chapter, take a minute to reflect on who you are and who or what shaped you to be the person that you are today.

Before we get started with the six steps of the *D.I.R.E.C.T Approach* let's start by finding out your definition of a leader. This will help you, as you go through the book, to focus on the parts of the approach that fit your leadership style. Although it is essential to incorporate all of the steps into your leadership approach, you will find that some steps will resonate with your style of leadership more than others. Please conduct the following self-awareness/self-assessment exercise that will focus you on clearly defining what leadership means to you and subsequently what it means to your team. Often times, those definitions are different and are the root cause of many issues within a team. So let's start by writing down your own definition of leadership. Pull out a sheet of paper and write, in your own words, what leadership means to you.

Now that you have described what leadership means to you I want you to take a minute and reflect on your own leadership style. Do you embody the definition that you wrote down? Be honest with yourself. If this is truly your definition of what a leader should be, are you that leader? It's important that you take some time now to really analyze this question. Are you the leader that you described in your definition, and if not, how could you change that? Should you change it?

Next, I want you to think of a famous leader, any leader. Who comes to mind? First, make a list of famous leaders and then a list of people that have affected your life, people that you, personally, consider to be leaders. Before you read on, take a minute to jot down your answer to this question.

Let's look at your famous leaders first, who did you write down? Was it JFK? Was it MLK? How about Lee Iacocca? Did you choose the Dalai Lama? Adolph Hitler? Margaret Thatcher? Queen Elizabeth II? It might have even been Harriet Tubman, Joan of Arc, Ronald Reagan, Donald Trump, Julius Caesar, or Jesus. It really doesn't matter who you named; it matters that YOU named them. Somewhere along the line you have decided or someone has told you that the person you named is a leader. The question is what makes them a leader?

So, now let's take a minute to identify what you think makes a good leader. Go back to the list you created and write down next to each name a leadership trait or characteristic or just a reason why you think that person was/is a good leader. If you wrote down a name because you were taught or told that the person was a good leader and you don't know why, that's ok – just say so. No one is grading you on this exercise. I do, however, encourage you to do some research on the people that you don't know and find out why they were thought to be effective leaders.

As an example of a famous leader you might list JFK and you might annotate as characteristics that he had a contagious spirit and he inspired the nation. An example of personal leaders may be your parents, and the trait or characteristic for their leadership may be that they are supportive, loving, and honest.

Now take a look at the list you created. Do the traits or reasons for what made or make your famous leaders effective look similar to what you think make or made your personal leaders effective? Maybe they are the same and maybe they aren't but one thing is for sure: The reasons you provided under the personal leaders are the traits that you think make up a good leader. These are traits that you look for in a leader and the traits you want your leadership to possess. Many people never really take the time to do an exercise like this to identify what right looks like to them. Ironically, many leaders make the mistake of failing in the exact areas that they feel are important in a leadership role. Take for instance the leader that respects her boss for acknowledging important family events and is understanding about allowing time off to attend these events. It is important to her to have a job and a boss that allows her time to spend with family but when it comes to her own team she is less than generous. She might require them to work nights and weekends to accomplish a project, thus reducing the amount of time they are able to spend with their own family.

The point of this exercise is for you to identify, specifically, what a good leader looks like to you. The exercise is meant to provide you not only awareness but an assessment of your own skills. Call it a "gut check," if you will, to see if you yourself are meeting your own expectations as a leader. As humans, we are more than happy to criticize and point out others' mistakes, yet when it comes to performing self-assessments, we fall short. So take some time to "look under the hood" and identify what parts of you need fine-tuning.

Now comes the tricky part. You have defined what leadership means to you, identified your leaders and their traits, and conducted an awareness/assessment exercise on what a good leader looks like to you. Guess what, your team might not list the same leaders or the same traits. That exercise was for you, and I strongly suggest that you conduct the same or a similar exercise with your team.

Your team members may have traits or characteristics on their list that you don't have on yours. Understanding what is important to your team members or more specifically understanding your team members will reduce the amount of conflict and make for a much better relationship. So, how do you find out what they think – YOU ASK THEM!

Throughout this book, I will discuss time-tested tools and techniques that will improve the overall effectiveness of your team. *D.I.R.E.C.T* is an acronym that will describe six essential steps for being an effective leader.

Step 1: **Develop Relationships**
Step 2: **Inspire Action and Support**
Step 3: **Recognize and Reward**
Step 4: **Empower and Educate**
Step 5: **Communicate and Counsel**
Step 6: **Take Care of Your Investment**

Skeptics and nonbelievers have referred to this leadership style as "warm and fuzzy," "touchy feely," and "soft," but the most accurate adjective is effective. One of the best things about this leadership approach is that anyone who genuinely cares about people can implement it. I have taught and trained these techniques to a variety of people with different leadership skills, different leadership styles, different personality types, and varying levels of experience and knowledge. I have implemented this style in the military and in the civilian sector, and it has proven successful across the board. Many were skeptical at first, but they were believers in the end.

H I N T :

Interacting with people humanly, empowering them to share their opinions, and mentoring them to grow personally and professionally doesn't make you weak; it makes you the leader that people want to work for and with.

CHAPTER 2:

I suppose leadership at one time meant
muscles, but today it means getting
along with people.

~ **Mahatma Gandhi**, leader of Indian nationalism ~

回回

START OFF STRONG

Growing up in Gilman, as I stated, it was a struggle to entertain ourselves, and sometimes in pursuit of entertainment, we
didn't make the best choices. I remember as a teenager, my best
friend and I decided to go to the county fair. We were wise and
mature beyond our years, at least that's what we thought, and
decided that it would be a good idea to take beer with us on
the drive and into the fairgrounds. As we drove into the
fairgrounds a policeman on his horse looked down into our
car, saw the beer, and promptly pulled us over. Keep in mind
that this was the summer in between our senior year of high
school and college, freshly graduated, our life in front of
us. Also keep in mind that I was 18 and my friend, whose
birthday wasn't until September, was 17; neither of us was of
legal drinking age, we had open alcohol in the car, and I was

driving. None of these things were really given a second thought. In our minds, they all seemed to be good choices. Also note that this was the 80's and the laws, restrictions and blood alcohol content level were much less than they are today.

I can't explain to you the fear that I experienced that day. We were taken to the Police tent inside the fairgrounds by the policeman who I of course knew because I worked with his wife at the local truck stop. Once we arrived we were also greeted by two auxiliary police, who were the parents of two of our classmates. So, as we sat on display for the world to see, the embarrassment was mortifying. I could hear the words of my mother's advice ringing in my ear; "Think before you do it! If you don't want it broadcast on the evening news or seen on the front page of the paper, then you probably shouldn't do it!"

I remember the mother of one of my classmates, the auxiliary policewoman, sitting with me and comforting me as I cried. Don't get me wrong, she gave me the stern "I'm disappointed in you" look that mothers give, but she was still there to calm me as I sat in fear wondering what was going to happen to my friend and me.

We sat in that tent for what seemed like hours until the arresting policeman came in to talk to us. In his hand he had four pieces of paper, all of them tickets; three for me and one for my friend. Illegal consumption, illegal transportation, and driving under the influence were the charges. He sat and painstakingly read each of them, described the charges, to what extent the charges were punishable, and the fine associated with each. Then, as my 95-pound frame sat sobbing in disbelief and fear he stopped, stared at me sternly, and said:

"Young lady, you're lucky that your grandfather is who he is. I'm going to tear these tickets up and let you go with a warning. I think you have learned your lesson. You need to go home and tell your dad what happened here today. When I see him at K & H tomorrow morning I'm going to ask him if he knows about this. If he tells me no, I will rewrite the tickets. Do you understand?"

I was an 18 year old kid who one year later joined the Army's Reserve Officer Training Program (R.O.T.C) at my college. I received a scholarship from the Army to pay for my college and 22 years later I consider that decision one that shaped my life. I would not have been admitted into the program or received the scholarship had that policeman not had mercy on me. More importantly, had my grandfather not impacted him in some way to respect him enough to honor him by letting me off with a warning and the scare of my life, I might not be writing this book. Was I wrong? Without a doubt. Did I learn something? Absolutely!

After leaving the fairgrounds that night I was thankful to be Fratie Strode's granddaughter more than ever before, but it got me thinking, what did he mean by "You're lucky that your grandfather is who he is?" At that time I knew my grandpa as the man that fell asleep in the recliner when I went to visit. He was 6 foot 3 and about 220 pounds with white hair, broad shoulders, a small belly, and an ornery grin, and he always smelled like the outdoors. I used to walk into the house, not without taking off my shoes of course, and kiss him on top of his head as he sat in his recliner. He always acted like he didn't like it but I know he did. I would sit on the couch and listen to him yell at the Cubs or the White Sox as he informed the coach or players how awful they were. He didn't hear very well, but I think sometimes he just used that as an excuse not to have to talk while his game was on. He was a man of faith, read the bible every day, and he loved my grandma's cooking; well to be honest, we all loved grandma's cooking. He wore bib overalls and either a short sleeve cotton shirt or a flannel shirt, depending on the season, almost every day of his life. My grandpa was a farmer. A hardworking man that took his seat amongst other farmers every morning at the truck stop, a man that helped other farmers when needed, attended sales and auctions, shared the yield of his garden with others, and mowed an occasional yard for someone who couldn't do it themselves. Then it dawned on me, he wasn't just my grandpa, he was a good man. He was a man who had impacted others enough to gain their respect and their friendship. Relationships matter, people matter!

Consider in this next chapter the impact that you have on others. How do your words, your actions, and your reactions shape the people that surround you? Are you just a boss or are you a mentor? Are you just a coworker or are you a friend? Are you just a subordinate or are you a role model? What words would people use to describe you?

Step 1: Develop Relationships

D.I.R.E.C.T is a leadership approach that can provide amazing results and forge great relationships and friendships. If you are one of those leaders that believe that relationships and friendships have no place in business or the work place then you should probably throw this book away or give it to a friend that would benefit from its content. However, if you want to learn and grow as a leader, expand your comfort zone, and improve the effectiveness of your team, then keep reading.

There are six steps to the *D.I.R.E.C.T Approach,* but I want to make it clear that once you get past Steps 1 and 2, the steps are not sequential. In other words, you don't have to accomplish Step 3 before Step 4 or Step 4 before Step 5. What you will find is that you will not only be accomplishing many steps at once, but you will frequently repeat steps as the situation dictates. However, it is important to achieve Step 1 before you can realize its full effect and have success at any of the other steps. Additionally, Step 2 needs to be communicated clearly before moving on to subsequent steps.

It's also important to note that several of the steps will bleed into others. For instance, Step 5, Communicate and Counsel, is a step all its own but you will see many references to communication throughout the other steps.

As you read through this chapter consider the leaders that impacted your life as well as what kind of leader you want to be.

Step 1, Develop Relationships, is the foundation for the *D.I.R.E.C.T Approach* and, in my opinion, the foundation of leadership as a whole. Without Step 1 you may make progress, but you will significantly hinder your team from accomplishing and achieving their individual potential and the overall potential of the team. The most important thing about this step is that it cannot be faked! Do not make the mistake of faking interest in your staff or your team. You must be genuine in order to obtain the full effectiveness of Step1.

> *Leadership is getting players to believe in you. If you tell a teammate you're ready to play as tough as you're able to, you'd better go out there and do it. Players will see right through a phony. And they can tell when you're not giving it all you've got.*

~Larry Bird, an NBA Hall of Famer states:

The number one key to a successful team is knowing and understanding the members of your team and making the most of their experience, knowledge, and creativity to create a mutually respectful, safe, trusting, and fun work environment. If you don't know who your team members are both personally and professionally, if you don't know how they learn, if you don't know what they think makes a good leader, if you don't know what they value, and maybe most importantly, if you don't know what motivates them, you will not be able to effectively utilize your team to their fullest potential.

Understanding their background, their successes, their failures, their home life, their personality, and their motivations will give you insight into each person and ultimately an advantage when determining how to best utilize them and their skills for the good of the individual, the team, and the organization.

> ***Effective leaders have the ability to consistently move themselves and others to action because they understand the "invisible forces" that shape us.***
>
> ~ Anthony Robbins, author and motivational speaker ~

Anthony Robbins philosophizes that we act the way that we do because of six human needs that shape our behavior. Similar to Abraham Maslow's Hierarchy of Needs, Robbins says that these six human needs define people's behavior.

> To listen to his TED performances go to http://www.theprofitshare.com/tony-robbins-six-human-needs/.

Robbins states that there are 6 Human Needs that everyone requires in order to be fulfilled, but some needs shape us more than others. The first four needs are what he calls the Needs of the Personality, and he says that everyone finds a way to achieve these. The achievement of these needs may not always be positive, but everyone finds a way to achieve them. For example; an uneducated teen with a poor home life and little money may find significance by pointing a gun at a store owner's head.

The last two needs are what he calls the Needs of the Spirit or how a person reaches fulfillment or Maslow's self-actualization step.

1. **Certainty** – the need for certain things to happen a certain way
2. **Uncertainty** – the need for variety and change
3. **Significance** – the need to feel significant
4. **Love and Connections** – the need to be loved or make connections with another
5. **Growth** – the need to grow
6. **Contribution** – the need to give to something bigger than ourselves

Just imagine for a minute the impact you could have if you knew your team well enough to know which need or needs shaped people's decisions. Consider how assigning tasks, recognizing performance, hiring team members, or building relationships would change if you took the time to determine which human need or needs were important to your team members.

●◆ Early in my career I attempted to motivate or inspire a certain "difficult" team member using reasoning associated to significance, only to learn later that his behavior was shaped by certainty. Upon discovery he became very productive and ultimately one of my top performers. Prior to me recognizing his top need, I was very frustrated with him and his performance

So, how do you discover what needs shape your team? It really isn't that difficult, believe it or not. Step 1, Develop Relationships, is the key to learning what it is that makes people tick. There are many ways to accomplish this step of the leadership approach, and in the next couple of chapters I will share with you a few successful techniques that I have used in the past.

The Initial Counseling:

Although counseling will be discussed more completely in Step 5, I think it is important for The Initial Counseling to be discussed in Step 1. The Initial Counseling is the first opportunity you have to begin developing your relationship with your new team member. This should be accomplished within the first week of new team member's joining your team. The purpose of this meeting is to discuss position description, duties, responsibilities, and your expectations for the team member.

During this meeting it's important that you clearly explain what success looks like for them and how their efforts contribute to the success of the team. For example, your conversation might go something like this: "You will be successful in this position if you exhibit a strong work ethic, contribute to the growth of the team, and continue to improve yourself. Your position is vital to the organization because you provide the knowledge, experience, and skills that we need and without you we would not be able to achieve our goals." Be specific in how his or her skills will improve the organization as well as what specific goals he or she can help the team achieve. These types of conversations clearly communicate to the new team member what you, the boss, need him or her to do to be successful. Clearly articulating this message; providing it in writing and documenting it in the file provides a vivid picture of what success looks likes and shows that the new member is a valued part of the team.

Additionally, during this Initial Counseling, use a portion of your time to learn about the person's family. This sends a message to the team member that you care about things other than work and plants a seed for later conversations. Not to mention that it provides you valuable information about your new team member's home life that will assist you in making future decisions. For instance, if you know that one of your new team members is a single Dad with an eight year old daughter at home, you should consider that when assigning tasks that keep him past the normal work day. Am I suggesting treating team members differently, I ABSOLUTELY, am! Team members are individuals: They don't have the same skills, the same attitudes, the same knowledge or the same home life. In order to insure that they are reaching their potential, you have to treat them as individuals for the good of the team. I will discuss this in depth in Step 2.

Fair doesn't always mean equal, not everyone is the same. Don't try to treat them as if they are.

~ Colonel Chris Lawson, U.S. Army ~

Do not rush or skip The Initial Counseling. Often managers pawn off new team members to a "sponsor" that will show them around and stay with them as a support system until the new team member is comfortable navigating on his or her own. Although this is a good practice, and I strongly suggest it, make sure the sponsor puts you on the schedule. Schedule a block of time specifically for this, not a drive by when the sponsor sees the line in front of your office has depleted. Make it clear that this interview is important to you, and schedule adequate time to conduct the counseling. Outside of the interview, this is your first conversation with your new team member; make it count.

In the Army, as a Company Commander, you are required to sign off on all new Soldiers' welcome packet. Similar to how I described above, all new Soldiers are given sponsors and taken around to each person in the chain of command that has an impact on their Army experience. They meet the people that pay them, supply them with uniforms, evaluate them, etc. Because of the numerous things that need to be accomplished during the course of the day, this task often gets "pencil whipped." Meaning that the task is accomplished if anyone checks the paperwork, but it certainly wasn't accomplished to the standard that it was intended to be accomplished.

Shortly after taking command of my company, the Readiness NCO (Non-Commissioned Officer) came to me with a stack of sponsorship packets and asked me to initial the commander block. Puzzled by this, I asked him when I would get the chance to talk to the new Soldiers. Just as puzzled he responded by informing me that "we normally don't bring them in to see you Ma'am (stammering and feeling awkward after seeing the look on my face), but we can if you would like us to."

I explained to the NCO that not only did I want to meet them but I wanted to spend some time with them to give what I called the big picture speech to ensure they knew where and how they fit in to our organization.

The emphasis that I placed on that meeting established the tone of my command and changed the atmosphere of the company. The fact that I took the time to meet, get to know, and share my command philosophy with every Soldier in my company showed my Soldiers that relationships were important to me and I wasn't willing to "pencil whip" my time with them.

       ●✧ Think back to your previous jobs and recall your first meeting with your new boss. Did you get one? You would be surprised at

the number of people who have told me that
they never met the person that evaluated
them. That's unacceptable. Also, how many
times did you get the opportunity to meet the
boss only to and walk out uninspired or unim-
pressed?

In some cases, depending on the profession or organization, this may be your first introduction to your new team
members. You may not have had the opportunity to interview
them, and if that is the case, this counseling becomes even
more important.

Ensure that you take time earlier in the day, prior to the
meeting, to review the new team member's file. In the event
that you were not the hiring official this will give you some
insight into your new team member's background. If you were
the hiring official it will give you an opportunity to jog your
memory about your new team member.

回 凹

H I N T :
**It's best to have an outline that you can
reference during The Initial Counseling.
The outline helps ensure you cover all the
information you want to discuss during
that meeting. This also ensures that The
Initial Counseling is standard for all of
your team members.**

回 凹

If you are a leader of a team that is already established, it's not too late to use this technique. Simply infuse this step into a regular counseling session with a team member. You could even apologize to your team members for not getting to it earlier and assure them that you will be conducting regular counseling in the future. This reinforces to them that this is important to you and the success of the organization.

Again, for new team members, this should take place within the first week of the team member joining the team or as soon as possible for current members that haven't had the opportunity to meet with you.

CHAPTER 3:

You can't shake hands with a closed fist.

~ **Indira Gandhi**, Former Prime Minister of India ~

回 回

THE ONE ON ONE CHAT

When I was a kid and even a young adult I remember going out to supper with my parents. Everything would be fine as we looked over menus and discussed what to order. Then, the waitress would come! I would sit there praying that Dad would just order his meal, we would order ours, and the waitress would go away only to be seen again when she delivered our food. As normal as that sounds, that never happened. You see, my Dad has this need to know everyone. I remember on several occasions being so embarrassed when my dad would ask the waitresses what seemed to me to be personal questions about their lives. Regardless of whether or not he knew them he would ask questions. "What's your name? Where are you from? How long have you lived here? Who's your dad?" That last question always led into a genealogy lesson that went something like this:

"Oh, I think I know him. His sister, Jan, was married to my cousin's son on my mom's side. Now, they aren't married anymore but their son, who I guess would be your cousin, he was a pretty good athlete wasn't he? What's his name? Sam? Anyway, his girlfriend and my son, Jeff, he's in the Air Force now, use to date."

Mortifying as a child! I used to want to crawl under the table and pretend I wasn't related. I was always amazed at the amount of information that these people would share with a complete stranger, but they always did. He has always had a connection to people. If I had to guess, I would say he gets it from his dad, who I have already established, impacted many people in his life.

What was even more amazing than their sharing their life story with a stranger was when we would go back to that restaurant a couple of months later, they remembered him, and he definitely remembered them.

The short amount of time that he spent getting to know them left an impression.

It's not uncommon for him to share nuggets of information that he has learned during the course of his day. When I ask where or how he came to know such information he confesses that it's a result of a conversation with the barber or a convenience store clerk or a Costco employee. He has done this as long as I can remember. He doesn't ask to be nosey; he asks because he genuinely likes people and wants to get to know them. He likes connecting the dots and understanding people, where they come from and where they are going. He loves hearing people's stories and connecting with them.

Again, I think it comes from the small town influence of knowing everyone. Although he hasn't lived in Gilman for over 25 years I think he still misses the connections that a small town provides.

As an adult and as a leader, it all makes perfect sense to me now. Making a connection with people, their lives, and their families forms a bond that others, without the connection, just don't have.

Step 1: Develop Relationships (continued)

It's important that you spend one on one time with your team members so they know that you care about them, their work, their family, and their lives. Consider the impact that my dad has on strangers, and imagine the impact that you could have on team members. If you take the time to get to know them as Dad did, imagine the response you will receive.

The one on one chat is not a time for counseling, although sometimes the opportunity for personal counseling might present itself during these chats. If at all possible keep this light, and if the conversation takes a turn to a more serious topic, relocate to a more private setting. This is simply a short conversation during the week when you "catch up" on things going on in your employee's life.

🔲🔲

H I N T :
One on One Chats do not have to be scheduled; it can be five minutes in the break room, a ride in an elevator, or a talk at the employee's desk.

🔲🔲

This chat is nothing fancy or scripted just a chat and face time with your team member. These short encounters and your acknowledgment of them validates for them that you know they exist and they are more than just an employee.

The conversation can range from "at-a-boys" to family. You could discuss with them hobbies, vacations, kids, spouses, current events, or sports. As I said, this is a short conversation that merely consists of the exchange of information for the purpose of developing a relationship.

This type of communication makes you more approachable in the future in the event that a team member has a more serious issue or concern that needs to be discussed with you. If this type of relationship is not developed there could be a fear or uneasiness that surrounds discussing important topics. The more comfortable people are talking to you the more comfortable the work environment is, the happier the team member. Happy team members equal effective and efficient teams.

Leadership is solving problems. The day soldiers stop bringing you their problems is the day you have stopped leading them. They have either lost confidence that you can help or concluded you do not care. Either case is a failure of leadership.

~ Colin Powell, Former United States Secretary of State ~

You should make an effort, if at all possible, to "chat" daily. A couple minutes out of your day will pay huge dividends for the team in the long term.

CHAPTER 4:

Build for your team a feeling of oneness, of
dependence on one another and of strength
to be derived by unity.

~ **Vince Lombardi**, Hall of Fame Football Coach ~

回 回

THE GROUP HUG

Shortly after 9/11 my unit was selected to deploy. Prior to our
deployment we were sent to our mobilization station, Ft.
Stewart, Georgia. While we were there I went to the Post
Exchange (PX) to pick up some things that I needed for the
deployment. As I was walking down one of the aisles I saw
a puzzle of the New York skyline, twin towers still standing.
It was a 1,000 piece puzzle that I bought as a reminder of why
we were deployed and the people that lost their lives on that
devastating day in our nation's history. Once we arrived at our
duty location, I pulled the puzzle out and put it in my office
where people would come in periodically to take a break and
help with the puzzle. It was a group project that the team
members worked on together. This type of group event builds

camaraderie and connects the group in a way that bonds you as a team. That puzzle was more than a break in the day or a group project; it stood for something much more. When it was finished one of my team members had it framed and it was presented to me as a special gift.

Step 1: Develop Relationships *(continued)*

Gather everyone in one location for a meet and greet. Create a fun "get to know you" exercise that serves a dual purpose for the team. For instance, you could introduce a new team member and acknowledge other team members for contributions during The Group Hug. Introduce a new team member to the team with a short biographical summary.

回凹

H I N T :
Make sure the new team member knows that you are going to share the information. The last thing you want is to start your relationship off with confidentiality or trust issues.

回凹

The summary will establish credibility for your new team members and make the transition quicker and easier than throwing them to the wolves to fend for themselves. It acts as an ice breaker and establishes or identifies commonalities with the existing team that may not have been known.

回回

H I N T :
The information for the biography can be
gleaned from the Initial Counseling.

回回

You could also ask the new team members to write some-thing up for you to read; thus allowing them to share what they want to share and getting a peek into their writing skills. You could assign another team member the responsibility and therefore encourage team members to share and talk to one another. The Group Hug works best when combined with introducing new members to the team so they can see where they fit into the equation. It allows them to meet everyone and network with their new teammates. Make it short, entertaining, and meaningful. Many people are annoyed by useless meetings so make sure the purpose is clarified and met.

The Group Hug can also be used as a break during the day. This allows team members to take a break from work and socialize with their peers without guilt. This could be a fresh air break, a quick game, or a walk.

回回

H I N T :
At one of my jobs I gathered everyone in
the center of the office a couple of times
a week and we played Bop It for 10-15
minutes.

回回

Any of these small, short activities that encourage team-work and build relationships are ideal for The Group Hug. These can be spontaneous or scheduled, but again the intent must be clear and communicated. Personally, I preferred them to be spontaneous. As a leader you will be able to gauge the mood of your team. It's important for as many team members as possible to attend. Very few things can't wait 10 or 15 minutes.

The Group Hug is best when you sense that the team needs a boost or a break. Regardless, you should try to make time for The Group Hug at least once a week.

CHAPTER 5:

Leadership is not about titles, positions
or flowcharts. It is about one life
influencing another. .

~ **John C. Maxwell**, author, speaker, leadership expert ~

回 回

THE SOCIAL GET
TOGETHER
(WITHOUT SPOUSES)

Recently, a former Army Officer and I were discussing getting
some of the old gang together from our former unit, the 634th
Brigade Support Battalion. After talking with him I decided to
create a Facebook page for our former Battalion. I went
through my list of "friends" and invited them to the page and
encouraged them to invite others. I posted some pictures and
inquired as to their interest in having a reunion and asked
them to share their fondest memory of the 634th.

After creating the page there was an outpouring of posts
and pictures and stories shared from former members, retirees,

and current members. All were fond memories of shared experiences that will stay with them for a lifetime.

There are currently over 300 members of the page, and it is still growing. As I sat and read the posts I grew nostalgic of the times we shared. Those Soldiers and Officers were not just members of the Illinois Army National Guard, but they were members of my family as I am a member of theirs. Those times that we spent away from the armory, out of uniform, were just as important as the times we were deployed with one another. Those bonds, those friendships, those shared experiences brought us together as people: people with common interests, people whose kids went to school together, people who would give up a Saturday afternoon to help pour concrete or roof a house or go to a wedding. People who celebrated birthdays and babies and helped mourn the death of loved ones. We laughed together, argued and competed amongst each other, and ultimately grew together as people and Soldiers.

Those memories are behind us, but those friendships are forever. Many of those experiences were the result of time spent outside of the work place, but that time together developed some of the strongest teams and friendships that I have had the pleasure of being a part of. The Social Get Together is a great way to accomplish this type of connection with your team.

In the end, all business operations can be reduced to three words: people, product, and profits. Unless you've got a good team, you can't do much with the other two.

~ Lee Iacocca, American Businessman ~

Step 1: Develop Relationships (continued)

The Social Get Together (without spouses) is an opportunity for you and the staff to socialize away from the office.

Although, inevitably, the conversation will probably revolve around work, it is a stress free environment that is safe and free from the physical constraints of the office. There are no meetings, phones, or emails to distract or keep a team member from participating. Placing people in a social environment reduces barriers of hierarchy and structure and provides a more relaxed atmosphere to get to know one another. This also provides an opportunity for you to appear "human" to your subordinates. It allows you to show your team members that there is more to you than deadlines, projects, and task lists.

This type of event not only allows you to get to know your team members better, but it allows coworkers to bond as well.

回 凹

H I N T :
An added benefit to these events, often times, is some great conversations that result in solutions and resolutions for issues in the work place. You will be surprised at the amount of work that gets accomplished in a "social" environment.

回 凹

The Social Get Together should not be a required event. It's essential that you set the environment as being a fun, open event for the purpose of decompressing, celebrating successes, and creating shared experiences. If you make the event required then it becomes labeled as "forced fun" and carries a negative connotation, then no one looks forward to it or wants to attend. Not only do people not look forward to it, they dread it and resent you for making them attend. This may mean several attempts where only a few people show but eventually the word will get out and participation will increase.

Schedule the event at least two or three weeks in advance in order to give your team members enough notice to make arrangements for them and their families. More advanced notice is better for all involved. Send out an e-mail and announce the event at staff meetings. Provide as much information as possible as to the event time, date, location, and activities. Again, ensure that there is an element of fun in the event to entice them to want to attend, if for nothing else but to have a good time.

回囘

H I N T :
Suggested venues for the Social Get Together are restaurants, social clubs, bowling alleys, or miniature golf courses. All of these locations provide a fun, social, relaxed environment that is conducive to meeting the objectives of the event

回囘

After the event, send out an email to the entire team thanking everyone for attending. This will entice others to ask questions about the event and eventually increase participation. Also, ask for suggestions for the next gathering. Asking for suggestions reinforces to them that their opinion matters and that this is an event for the team.

These events should be held at least quarterly and if possible on the heels of a success for the team. I will discuss this more in Step 3.

CHAPTER 6:

A man should never neglect his family
for business.

~ **Walt Disney**, American Film Maker ~

回 凹

THE SOCIAL GET
TOGETHER
(WITH SPOUSES)

When I was the Executive Officer I had a fairly new employee who had never been able to convince his wife to go to the annual ball, where Soldiers and their dates would come together for an evening of "fun and fellowship." I convinced him to ask her to attend our annual ball and ensured him that he and his wife would have a good time. He did, she came, and they did. During the event I spoke to his wife, and she said to me:

I'm so glad that you had John ask me; I've never really understood what he does or cared to get to know the people he does it with\, but you guys are a lot of fun. I'm glad I came, thanks.

Prior to that night she would suffer through his stories about work because she didn't know the people he was referring to. She was annoyed when he was gone and uncertain as to what he was doing. One night shared with people and spouses of the organization changed her opinion and her attitude.

Family is part of the equation, if not the most important part, of every employee's life. Include them in your team, and everyone wins.

Step 1: Develop Relationships (*continued*)

The Social Get Together (with spouses) is almost imperative if you are in an organization which is a) Coed or b) spends time throughout the year working on projects that take time away from the employee's family. Involving the spouses allows them to meet you and the other members of the team. This also allows them to learn who their spouses are spending time with when they are not at home. In addition, when you hold an event that invites the family they become a part of the team. They are more likely to understand time spent away from family if they feel like they are part of the success of the team. This type of an event also provides an opportunity to garner relationships and build friendships among coworkers and their spouses.

If your team is in various locations this event works best when combined with a team or company event. If it is feasible, schedule a training conference, outside of the office, in combination with The Social Gathering. This will alleviate or significantly reduce the cost to the team members because the company will be footing the bill for lodging and possibly meals and transportation. If executed properly you can accomplish training during the day and The Social Gathering in the evening.

回回

H I N T :
An added benefit to this option is increased attendance at The Social Gathering. The team members will already be in attendance for the required training and therefore more likely to attend The Social Gathering.

回回

It can be an excuse to leave the kids with the grandparents and have a night out with adults. Try to hold the event near someplace fun so the spouses have plenty of things to do while employees are in training. A casino, a large city, golf course, or the beach are great locations to hold these.

If your team is all in one location then make a day out of the event. A sporting event is perfect for this. Other venues that would work are golf outings, shopping trips, fundraisers, or volunteer projects. Any event that brings everyone together to socialize and have fun is going to be a winner

Similar to The Social Gathering (without spouses), The Social Gathering (with spouses) should not be a required event. However, if marketed correctly, this will be an event that team members and spouses look forward to year after year. You can make them as casual or as formal as you want as long as the key element of fun is incorporated into the theme. The Social Gathering (with spouses) is a great time to recognize exceptional performers or teams as well as spouses. This will be discussed more in depth in Step 3.

These events should be scheduled semi-annually. Schedule far enough in advance so families can plan for the event.

After reading this chapter you may be thinking that the last thing you want to do is to spend time with people from work, outside of work. Why would I want to subject myself to more time with people from work? I don't even like some of them. So, to suggest spending more time with them may seem a bit too much. You may be thinking that the time spent away from the office is reserved for your family and you don't have additional time to be planning parties and get-togethers because you take too much time away from your family already. All of these are valid concerns, but I will tell you that you will have to do some of these things in order to fully develop effective, constructive relationships with your team.

It honestly doesn't take much time during your day to initiate these relationships and plan the events associated with them.

CHAPTER 7:

I really want to see us build a product that lets you really feel a person and understand what's going on with them.

~ **Mark Zuckerberg**, Co-founder of Facebook ~

回 凹

ADDITIONAL RELATIONSHIP BUILDERS

Shortly after I started a new job two of my staff members "friended" me on Facebook. After a couple of weeks one of them who was "stalking" my page learned that I owned my own business. He inquired about it, we discussed it, and he was able to learn something about me that I had not previously shared. In addition, he learned that we had mutual friends, and that sparked a conversation as well. Facebook is One on One chat material for days!

Step 1: Develop Relationships *(continued)*

Social Media

One of the quickest ways to get to know your employees is by being "friends" or "followers" with them on social media sites such as Facebook or Twitter. I would however caution you about initiating those "friendships." You don't want to appear as though you are spying or checking up on them, so I would wait for them to invite you as opposed to the other way around. If you aren't comfortable sharing that level of personal information with your team then only share the parts you want, there are normally privacy settings that will allow you to customize your information. I will tell you, though, the more "human" you are the more likely you will successfully connect with your team.

◙ ◙

H I N T :
Social media allows you to learn information about your employees or team members that can be discussed during your One-on-One Chats.

◙ ◙

These types of sites identify common interests as well as common friends and can be facilitators in developing a stronger relationship with your team members.

Also, some social media forums have a format for creating specific pages for specific groups of people. You could create a page specifically for your team, department, or organization. This page could be used to upload photos from social gatherings, send invitations to social events, or simply share ideas or network with others on the team. You could create it yourself or task someone on your team to maintain the page.

Many social media sites also share birthdays, spouse and family information, and hobbies. These can serve as reminders for you to wish them happy birthday, plan a get together, or send a card. Again, you can use the team page to communicate some of this information. Photographs can be used to put together slide shows for retirement, promotion, or transfer events.

All in all it's a great way to learn and share information for the entire team.

Team Building Events:
Team Building Events are great motivators and can be a lot of fun if planned appropriately. They are great for getting to know your team, how they interact, react, problem solve, and communicate. Team Building Events provide education, knowledge, and inspiration and connect team members in a way that other work activities do not. I will discuss this more in depth in Step 2, but Team Building Events should occur annually at a minimum.

As always, these events should have a fun component built into them as well as lessons that make the team stronger and more productive. As with all events of this nature it's important to state the objectives and goals of the event so the participants have a clear understanding of your intent.

Personality Tests:
Some organizations have the funding to administer personality tests to their employees that help them understand each person's specific personality, learning style, or characteristics. It's a fun exercise to do at a conference and really puts things into perspective when it comes to the way people think.

The <u>Myers Briggs Type Indicator</u> is probably the most popular, but there are others as well. If you haven't taken it, I would recommend you do so. These types of assessments or tests will produce "a ha" moments for the entire team. These assessments will prove beneficial across the team and create an understanding for all.

It's been my experience, having taken many of these assessments, that they will identify four main types of people or personalities. Each assessment has different names or titles for the categories, below is my version:

1. **The Doer:** Make a decision, even if it's wrong. If it's wrong I'll make another decision, but let's get this ball rolling. Likes to be in control. Mission oriented. Very dependable, timely, schedule oriented, not concerned about making friends but about accomplishing tasks.

2. **The Entertainer:** Concerned more about building relationships, making friends, and planning for what's going to happen after the job is done. This is your party planner. Everyone loves them but they can be a little scatter brained and unfocused. Creative, energetic, crowd pleaser, untimely, procrastinator. A leader that others will follow out of pure curiosity.

3. **The Wall Flower:** Go with the flow, do as their told. Don't like conflict. Rule followers. Don't color outside the lines. Dependable, always meets deadlines and always comes to work on time or early. Not decision makers, in fact cringes at the thought of making a decision.

4. **The Nerd:** Want to be left to do their own thing and not be disturbed. Give them a task to do and get out of their way. Give these people a manual or a checklist and watch them

excel. Focused, uninterested in people or office politics. Disconnected from big picture but very efficient and proficient in producing their part.

Similar to Anthony Robbins' Six Human Needs, if you can figure out which one of these categories your team members relate to you will have better success managing your team and getting the most out of them.

Summary

The eight ideas in the previous chapters are an example of the ways that you can get to know your staff, individually. I cannot stress enough that this attempt to better understand and get to know your team cannot be phony! If you don't care about them, their family, or their lives don't try to fake it. They will see right through it, and that will have tragic results.

> *Don't compromise yourself. You are all you've got.*
>
> ~ Janis Joplin, Singer, Songwriter ~

Also, do not expect this to happen overnight, and do not expect everyone to be as open to getting to know each other. Especially if this is something completely opposite of anything they have ever seen from you, they will be skeptical of your motives or question your authenticity. Many leaders also make the mistake of using a "universal" style in order to get to know their subordinates. In other words they use the same approach with every member of their team, regardless of age, culture, personality, or experience. Be aware that you will probably have to change your technique, depending on the person, in order for him or her to trust you and believe you are genuine. Some people aren't comfortable in a social environment, and yet others aren't comfortable sharing personal details about themselves. You will have to find the formula that works for each of your team members and establish a unique relationship with each of them. It may take longer for you to establish trust with one team member than another, but don't give up.

CAUTION:
Don't force it; there is a formula for everyone if you are willing to put in the time and effort to discover it.

Understand that without a solid foundation, the remaining steps of the *D.I.R.E.C.T Approach* are more difficult to achieve.

Think of the *D.I.R.E.C.T Approach* as a dart board with all the steps located around the board and Step 1 as the bull's eye. It takes practice, aim, patience, and a plan to hit the bull's eye, but it scores you the most points, and ultimately you need to hit it to win. Too many leaders attempt to throw darts at the board with no plan and hope to hit something that sticks. Almost anyone can close their eyes, throw a dart in the general direction of the board, and hit something. Unfortunately this is how some leaders go through the process; sometimes they get lucky and hit something that is important. In order to consistently hit the bull's eye you have to focus, practice, aim, and make a plan. You won't hit the bull's eye on your first try, and you won't connect with your team on the first try, but if you use the *D.I.R.E.C.T Approach* you will be consistent and achieve results faster than if you close your eyes and hope something sticks.

CHAPTER 8:

Good actions give strength to ourselves
and inspire good actions in others.

~ **Plato**, Greek Philosopher ~

回凹

PURPOSE, DIRECTION, AND MOTIVATION

During my career I have encountered many different types of leaders. Arrogant leaders, selfish leaders, incompetent leaders, bull headed leaders, micromanagers, hands off leaders, and bullies, to name a few. Thankfully I have also had the pleasure of interacting with inspiring, visionary, and motivational leaders.

Unfortunately, on one occasion I encountered an arrogant, selfish, bull headed, micromanaging, bully. This guy was convinced that because of his position he had all of the answers. He wouldn't entertain anyone's ideas or input except his own and insisted on opposing experienced, knowledgeable advisors. He was consistently challenged because he refused to take guidance or direction from anyone beneath him in the food chain and because of his position bullied everyone to get his way. He was confrontational and quoted rules and regulations as gospel when it suited his purpose but manipulated them to his benefit every chance he got.

He was productive; I'll give him that. He got the job done, but the cost we paid in the process was unacceptable. He was loathed! I don't mean people disliked him but understood the position he was in; I mean he was hated! There were more complaints against this leader than every other leader combined. The turnover in his organization was the highest and the morale the lowest. His subordinates began sabotaging him, and the productivity decreased exponentially. He was losing good people as soon as they could jump ship.

That was several years ago, and do you know that one of his subordinates told me just the other day she still can't stand to be in the same room with him. I haven't been around him recently but apparently he hasn't changed much and is still an arrogant, selfish, bull headed, micromanaging bully. Unfortunately, some people never learn.

CAUTION:
Productivity is only part of the equation; without the skills to manage people and inspire action and support, your leadership becomes a dictatorship.

Step 2 – Inspire Action and Support

Humans want to know WHY they are doing something, and it has to be for a better reason than a paycheck. The "because I said so" answer only works with team members that have little to no ambition to grow or to be part of the solution. Leadership by intimidation or fear does not promote a safe, fun, productive work environment. Resentment, apathy, and discontent are the result of leadership by intimidation, and this type of leadership produces disgruntled team members constantly looking for other opportunities and work environments. As a leader, you must clearly provide a purpose, direction, and motivation to accomplish a task, goal, or vision. This clear direction inspires them toward action and encourages them to support the goals and vision of the team and organization.

The years of an employee being loyal to an employer, a team, or leader/manager are long gone. Employees are constantly looking for a better salary, a better work environment, better hours, more benefits, and personal growth. It used to be that employees would be content going to a job day in and day out and performing their duties as assigned. They were content to trade long term loyalty to the company for minimum pay raises, middle management promotions, and eventually a pension. In today's work place, most employees don't stay with a company for 20-plus years like they did in the old days. Sure, promotions and pay raises are still enticing, but today inspiration, personal growth, job satisfaction, and training are the keys to longevity for most employees. If these are not received, team members will pursue other employment that provides them with these opportunities.

Providing team members with clear purpose, direction, and motivation increases the understanding of the project and reduces the time it takes to accomplish the action. It's really quite simple and doesn't take a whole lot of time to do, but the payoff is amazing.

Let's take a situation where you want your team or a person on your team to create a new system that can track your clients more efficiently than the one you're using now. You gather the person or people to accomplish the task, and you tell them, "I need you to create a new database for our clients. Get with the Information Technology department to help design it. I need it by the first. There is a bonus in it for you if you get it done sooner." This is an example of the "because I said so" method or a transactional leader approach. A transactional leader relies on rewards to accomplish a task. They help the follower identify what must be done to accomplish the desired result and provide resources to complete the task. However, a transactional leader does not provide motivation outside of self-interest and job security. In the example above, the team member knows that there is already a system that tracks the clients, and you haven't provided any information about why the old one isn't working or what you want the new one to do. You have simply provided a task with no purpose or direction and little motivation. They may not ask you, but they will talk amongst themselves and question why they are spending time creating something that already exists. They will waste time trying to figure out what you want and probably struggle, from fear of appearing incompetent, before asking for additional guidance.

CAUTION:

There are plenty of unpopular decisions that you will have to make as a leader; don't create an opportunity to be unpopular when you can avoid doing so with simple instruction and guidance.

Let's use the same scenario but word it differently and take the approach of a transformational leader: "I need you to work with the Information Technology department to create a new database for our clients that will allow us to create a method for maintaining historical records, create client contact information that can easily be accessed and merged for correspondence, and create statistical reports quickly and easily for our monthly reports. This system, when complete, should make all of our jobs easier. I picked you specifically for this task because of your database knowledge and because I know you can do this. I need the first draft of the system by next Friday and the finished product by the first of next month. Do you have any questions about what I need you to do?" Admittedly, this dialogue seems very robotic but you get the picture. This method provides the purpose, direction, and motivation needed to inspire action and support. First, it takes away the WHY we are creating a system when the old one works fine and tells them you are going to make their job easier (purpose). Second, you tell them exactly the components that you want the new system to have, give them the ability to ask questions to clarify your intent, and provide a timeline to accomplish the task (direction). Third, and most important, telling them that you picked them specifically lets them know you have faith in their ability and inspires them to action (motivation). A transformational leader motivates followers to work for achievement and self-actualization, not job security. They are able to express a clear vision and inspire others to accomplish the vision.

It is a terrible thing to see and have no vision

~ Helen Keller, American author ~

In this scenario you are addressing many of the 6 Human Needs, described by Anthony Robbins and discussed earlier; contribution is one of the needs of the spirit. You have told them that their contribution will make others' lives easier. They are contributing to something other than themselves. You have also provided the needs of certainty by telling them exactly what you want and when you want it. Uncertainty is addressed by giving them a task outside of their normal work load and the ability to work outside of the team with the Information Technology department. You have made them feel significant by telling them that you hand selected them to complete the task and love and connection by telling them that you have faith in their abilities or that you trust them. Growth is also a possibility if this project is something that they have never done before; by completing it they will learn and grow from the experience.

As you can see, by providing purpose, direction, and motivation you are able to relate the task to one of their 6 human needs even if you don't know which one shapes their behavior.

回回

H I N T :

Although money, reputation, and status should all be enough to inspire a team member to greatness, it just isn't so. How many times have you spoken to a coworker that is leaving the organization and in saying their goodbyes he says, "I won't miss the job but I'll miss the money or the reputation or the status."? Now, think about how many times you have heard people say, "I won't miss the job, but I'll miss the people."? Relationships and people motivate and inspire at a much higher level than money and status. Providing purpose, direction, and motivation inspire and develop loyal, hardworking, dedicated team members.

回回

Get Out of Your Office

As much as many leaders, supervisors, and managers would like it to be true, you can't be a leader from behind your desk!

You know exactly what and who I'm talking about. Everyone has experienced a boss that spent 90 percent of their time in her office, only to emerge for a crisis, lunch, a cup of coffee, or a bathroom break. These leaders have not learned the art of inspiration, delegation, or support.

CAUTION:
Don't be the guy/gal that sits in your office all day expecting your team to function flawlessly and only emerge to reprimand them for mistakes that they have made in your "absence."

With the technologies of today it's easy to get inundated with email and forget that there is a world outside of the computer monitor that sits in front of you. You have to fight the urge to communicate with your team via email. I will discuss this further in Step 5, but just remember people are inspiring, not email and not computers.

CHAPTER 9:

The best praise is done soon, specifically,
sincerely, personally, positively, and proactively.
A simple praise conveys "I saw what you did,
I appreciate it, here's why it's important,
and here's how it makes me feel"
– a lot of punch in a small package.

~ **Dr. Bob Nelson**, Author of 1001 Ways to
Reward Employees ~

回 凹

THANK YOU,
MAY I HAVE ANOTHER?

When I was a young officer our unit was on a field training
exercise, and Soldiers were instructed to dig a two person fighting position, a foxhole, to standard. We were establishing
a perimeter defense in our area of operation in preparation for
"enemy action" according to the intelligence report that we
received earlier that day. As I walked the perimeter I came
upon a particularly impressive fighting position. It was the
right depth, deep enough so the Soldier's armpits would rest on
the top lip of the foxhole. It was the right width, six and one

half feet wide. It had appropriately placed grenade sumps – a place to throw a grenade so it would explode in a hole rather than the foxhole. In the absence of sand bags they had used the dirt from the hole to create a barrier around the foxhole, designed to protect the occupants from shrapnel or ammunition. They had built steps into the side of the foxhole so they could easily exit if needed. They used rotted railroad ties that they found nearby to place on top of the dirt to provide added protection and to use as a base for overhead cover. They tied their ponchos together and tightly tucked them in between the railroad ties to provide protection from the rain as well as to provide a tarpaulin to lay foliage on to disguise the fighting position. They had clearly defined sectors of fire staked off inside the foxhole for each Soldier and had a range card that indicated where their line of fire started and where the adjacent foxholes began, providing them with a clear picture of the intersecting lines of fire and their section defensive plan. The whole project took no less than six hours for two Soldiers.

As I was standing there admiring the foxhole and praising the two Soldiers that dug it, their Commander walked by. I asked him to come and take a look at what a great job the two Soldiers had done. With little to no enthusiasm, he walked over to take a look.

As one of the Soldiers was in the middle of briefing their Commander on the amenities of his foxhole, a vehicle drove into our area. The Commander turned around, taking his attention off the Soldier and completely ignoring him as he was briefing. After what seemed to be an extended period of time and noticing that the Soldiers were becoming impatient at being ignored, I asked the Commander, "Sir, is that someone you need to go see? Private Smith and Private Jones can finish briefing you later." He stared at the vehicle for a few more seconds waiting to see who emerged from it and responded "No, it's *just* a rifle bearer."

As I stood in front of him with my rifle draped over my shoulder and then looked next to me to the two Soldiers standing in front of him with their rifles on their shoulders, it dawned on me what he meant. In the military only senior officers or Commanders carry a pistol, all others carry rifles. Annoyed by his arrogance and disregard for his audience I said "Does that mean rifle bearers aren't important enough to talk to, Sir?" I stated it respectfully and with a little smirk hoping he would get the hint and redeem himself to the three rifle bearers standing before him. I was attempting to give him "an out" to save face with the Soldiers. He didn't pick up on my hint or didn't care because his response to my question was "not important enough for me to stop what I'm doing and go talk to them." The two Soldiers, as offended as I was, cut their briefing short and went on about their duties.

All that Commander had to do was pay attention for five minutes, give an enthusiastic at-a-boy, and go about the rest of his day. Instead, when he finally gave it, his praise was less than genuine, he ignored them, and then he insulted them.

Kind words accompanied with well-timed attention are really not that difficult to spare. Those Soldiers and I formed a negative opinion of that officer that day that would take a significant amount of effort to reverse. He lost the respect of three of his subordinates within 15 minutes, all because of a few words.

Step 3 — Recognize and Reward

Recognition and reward are such easy things to do, and yet many organizations or leaders just don't do them. There are so many simple ways to weave this into your leadership philosophy and they cost little or nothing to implement. Let me first say that if you don't have some type of recognition program for your team or in your organization it's not too late. Actually, you could be a hero soon if you just implement some of the ideas that I share here. Recognizing your team members tells them that you appreciate them. How hard is it to just tell someone she is doing a good job? It's not hard at all. Don't you like to be appreciated? Showing or speaking your appreciation to a team member can be accomplished with little or no cost, but the value it has to your team member will be received as a lavish gift.

Telling or showing people that they are appreciated reinforces to your team that their hard work and dedication to the organization do not go unnoticed. By acknowledging them you are telling them that they make a difference to the success of the team and the organization.

There are many different ways to show your appreciation, but I'm going to share with you some of my favorites. They are easy to do, inexpensive, and require little or no coordination to execute.

Verbal Acknowledgment:
The verbal acknowledgement of an action is the easiest way to let people know that you are proud of them or they have done a great job. This can be accomplished either publicly or privately depending on your team member.

回回

H I N T :
Some team members "say" they don't want the attention, but I'm here to tell you that no one ever died by being publicly recognized for a good thing (well, I'm not 100% sure about that but pretty sure).

回回

Public Recognition:
There are many different venues for recognizing someone publicly, and depending on the accomplishment you may want to have levels of recognition in place. Some team members just need to know they are doing a good job. Again, as I spoke about in Step 1, this is just one more reason it is important to get to know your team members. You will learn their comfort level in relation to public recognition, their need or want for validation, what they value, and many more things that will assist you when recognizing and rewarding their performance.

Here are a few examples of a verbal public acknowledgment:

- At a staff meeting in front of peers
- During "The Group Hug"
- At a conference or an annual event (Social Get Together)
- At an awards banquet or during a high profile event
- In front of YOUR boss or the hierarchy of the organization
- A "drive by" their desk with a simple "great job" or "I'm proud of you" or "thanks for your help."
- In front of their subordinates

Some team members like to get a small award to signify they have done a good job.

Here are examples of tangible, nonverbal rewards or recognition:

- Mass email to team and hierarchy acknowledging accomplishment
- A letter of appreciation for their personnel file
- Time off
- Incentive pay
- A parking spot for a week

- A gift card
- Lunch with you
- Their name on a plaque

Some team members thrive on status.
Here are examples of status recognition and rewards:

- Give the team member more responsibility by putting him in charge of a task or possibly other team members
- Move to a bigger office
- Sit at the "big kids" table in your absence
- Provide a training opportunity
- Give a promotion

Again, the key is knowing your team members and knowing what they would prefer. Not everyone will be motivated by or want the same thing. One person may love to walk in the office and see his name on a plaque, where as another would rather have four hours off work. There is nothing wrong with giving them choices and letting them choose their reward. It's essential, when developing a rewards and recognition program that it is fair. By packaging a group of rewards and allowing members to choose their own reward, you ensure the system is fair for all.

回 凹

H I N T :
Make sure that you make the rewards something they actually want. In order to ensure that you are giving awards they actually want, ask them. Put together a list of items, tell them how many they can choose and ask them for other

suggestions. By asking for their input you assure that the recognition or reward is worth striving for, and you let them know that you value their opinion. If you create a rewards program in a vacuum without any input you risk providing rewards that no one cares about; employees won't work as hard to achieve the recognition.

回回

Celebrate your successes as a team when it makes sense, but always recognize your top performers even when celebrating as a team. Single out those that did an outstanding job instead of just lumping everyone together and giving equal credit to all members of the team. We all know that there are stars that you cannot accomplish tasks without; recognize them! Ignoring the contributions of top performers could put the team at risk. They may no longer perform or perform less than they once did. Even the most dedicated team members will stop working as hard as they normally did if their efforts aren't recognized, or worse they will leave the organization or the team for a more fulfilling position.

CAUTION:
Similar to mass punishment, team members are desensitized by mass praise.

Also, acknowledging the top performers incites a constructive competition amongst the team to strive for the recognition. Although as a general rule you accomplish more by cooperating with people than by competing against them, a little competition never hurts. In addition, it identifies potential mentors for younger or less experienced team members.

Recognizing top performers clearly identifies for the entire team that you value hard working, talented team members. In the event that the recognition and reward program was not communicated to all team members, now they know it exists and that their efforts will be rewarded. However, again, it is important to recognize the entire team's efforts because very few people are a success (or a failure) all by themselves. Acknowledging the team's efforts reinforces the need to continue to work together to accomplish goals.

Recognition and appreciation are not reserved for just your team. Do not forget to recognize other departments, support staff, and spouses; it's just the right thing to do. Just because someone is not on your team doesn't mean that he didn't contribute to the success of the team. This is especially important when recognizing spouses. Your team member spends an exorbitant amount of time either at work, doing work at home, or thinking about work. All of this takes time away from the family and increases the work load of the spouse. Recognize this support!

Acknowledging other departments builds alliances and expands the reach of the team and their resources. You may want to use the talents of others, outside your own team, to assist in a training event or for institutional knowledge. Building these relationships and recognizing their support will increase the effectiveness of your own team. Besides, acknowledging people for their efforts feels good to you and them. Do it just to make someone's day. Maybe it is the first time they have heard encouraging words.

> **Kind words can be short and easy to speak, but
> their echoes are truly endless.**
> ~Mother Teresa, Roman Catholic Nun~

CHAPTER 10:

Never tell people how to do things. Tell them
what to do and they will surprise you with their
ingenuity..

~ **General George S. Patton**, General, U.S. Army ~

回回

TRUST YOUR TEAM

I once had a woman who worked for me that came to work
every day, did her job quietly, rarely interacted with anyone,
and then went home. She was a little bit of an outsider, and
honestly she was picked on by some of her peers. She didn't
speak in staff meetings, even when asked for her opinion, and
never offered suggestions. She rarely complained or challenged
any decision, and she performed her job to standard. I sat
down with her one day and asked her why she never shared
her opinion or offered suggestions. Her answer:

Because it doesn't matter what I think, you're the boss.

I had clearly failed her as a leader. If she thought that was
my leadership philosophy then I did something to make her
think that. Even if I had told her otherwise, she didn't receive

the message or believe the content of the message. Either way, I had failed her.

She came from the old school mindset of only speak when spoken to and was not eager or interested in sharing any opinions. She was only interested in doing her job, whatever way she was told to do it, and going home at the end of the day. She would fall under "The Wall Flower" category that I mentioned earlier. I told her that I valued her opinion and asked for input not just for me but for the entire team. She had been there for several years and outlasted many that came before her, and I knew that she had insight and opinions that could be beneficial to the group. I told her that others may have similar issues and concerns but if they weren't addressed or shared I would never know about them and couldn't fix them.

She was pessimistic at first, but I convinced her to consider sharing her thoughts from time to time. A couple of staff meetings later, when asked for her issues she provided something small, but a contribution none the less. She gave me an antagonistic smirk as if to say "there, are you happy?" I acknowledged her smirk with one of my own and resolved her issue; from that point forward she provided her opinion, unsolicited most times. She presented a problem, I fixed it, and she trusted me. She trusted me to not embarrass her in front of the team when she shared an idea; she trusted me to work toward resolving an office issue, a personal issue, or a team issue. Most importantly, she trusted me when I told her that she was a valuable member of the team and believed me when I told her I wanted her input. I gave her a voice, and she became part of the team. Rarely, from that point forward, was she on the outskirts of the team.

Trust is a difficult thing to gain, yet so easy to lose. Empowering team members to act, react, create, and lead shows them that you have faith in them to perform a task on your behalf or in your absence. Acknowledging to them that you trust them will get you one step closer to them putting their trust in you.

We almost always find that when a person is made to feel like a part of a team that they will give more to the team. I conducted a management culture study for an organization to determine the effectiveness of training and mentorship programs throughout their organization. As part of the study I asked the respondents "Do you believe your supervisor is an effective leader?" Of those surveyed, 71 percent answered yes. When those 71 percent were asked why they believed their supervisor was an effective leader, 57 percent responded, "My opinion matters, and I am empowered to participate in team and organizational discussions."

Very rarely will you encounter a team member that just wants to be left alone or not included as part of the team. Often when you run across that person it's because he has never experienced inclusion before. These team members have never been asked their opinions or when asked their opinions were ignored or dismissed. They, more than likely, have never been told how they fit into the vision of the team. They trudge along on a daily basis doing the job that they are asked to do with little or no input into the bigger picture. They do this because they don't know any different.

回回

H I N T :
If you find a team member that truly wants to be left alone and won't interact with the team even after attempts of inclusion, then there is probably something else going on, a bigger challenge

that will need to be addressed in order
for you to receive full participation and
cooperation to the team.

冋 凵

Step 4 – Empower and Educate

Empower them

How do you empower team members? There are several techniques; the chapters that follow are the techniques that
I believe to be keys to your success. You will notice that these
techniques go hand and hand with what we discussed in Step
2, Inspire Action and Support.

    As a leader it is imperative to delegate responsibility and
solicit assistance from your team, your peers, and your supervisors. You cannot do everything on your own, and if you try
you will limit the amount of success possible for you, your
team, and the organization. When you are faced with new
projects, changes in policy and procedures, research, presentations, or simple tasks, approach them as a team. This technique will reduce stress, equalize the work load, involve
everyone in the process, breed accountability, and provide an
assessment tool to evaluate your team. In addition, when you
work together as a team, you celebrate successes as a team,
and that increases morale.

    Mutual trust is key to empowering your team. If you don't
trust them you can't empower them, and if they don't trust you,
your attempts at empowerment will be wasted. Trust is essential to any successful relationship.

回 凹

H I N T :
Your level of trust is equal to your level of influence.

回 凹

If you are one of those people who believes no one can do the job as well as you, you're going to spend many late nights in your office, alone, and you will have a team whose potential will never be realized. So what if it's not exactly like you want it? Those are opportunities for mentorship and growth. Either spend the time training your team, or do it all yourself; your choice. I promise you, though, if you take the time to train them they will learn your way, or you may learn a better way together. But first you have to give them the chance to try and trust that they have the skills and knowledge to accomplish the task. You never really know if you can trust someone until you find out that you can't. Take the chance to trust your team; they will normally surprise you with their results.

CHAPTER 11:

The ear of the leader must ring with the voices
of the people.

~ **Woodrow Wilson**, 28th President of the United States ~

回己

LET THEM BE HEARD!

When I became a Company Commander, I took over a
Company that was at 77% strength, and of those 28% were not
planning on re-enlisting or fulfilling the full term of their
contract. In addition there were 6% in danger of being
discharged due to medical issues, failed drug tests, or failing to
meet physical fitness, height, and weight standards. Making
matters worse, we didn't have a unit recruiter, so there were
no projected new recruits in our future. So, when I took over
the company it was at 77%, but if I didn't do something fast I
would be down to 43% in a matter of months.

My First Sergeant and I decided that the very first thing we
needed to do was to speak directly to the Soldiers and get some
answers from them. We split the company in half by separat-
ing all the "leadership" into one group and all the "followers"
into another.

In the military we call Soldiers who have a leadership position an Officer or a Non Commissioned Officer (NCO). Enlisted Soldiers are those that are not in a formal leadership position. Enlisted Soldiers and NCOs make up the enlisted rank structure, and Warrant Officers and Officers are part of the commissioned rank structure. Commissioned Officers outrank Non Commissioned Officers and enlisted Soldiers.

I talked to half of the company, and my First Sergeant talked to the other half. We asked them pointed questions about their experience in the unit and asked them to identify three things they liked and three things they didn't like. We made it clear to them that their feedback was important and explained to them that everything and everyone was fair game for the conversation. We also told them the purpose for our questioning was to improve the unit and grow as a team. Below are some of the issues that were addressed during our meeting:

- Training is boring; we do the same thing every drill.
- We have to sit around at the end of drill and wait for the Officers and NCOs to get done with their meetings before we can leave.
- I don't even know why we do some of the things that we do; what is the point?
- I joined the Guard to be part of something bigger. When my friends ask me what I do I say I fuel trucks. Not very impressive.

There were many more but the gist of it boiled down to them being bored, not working together as a team, and not understanding the bigger picture of what their jobs meant to the company, the battalion, and the brigade.

After listening to their issues and concerns we made them a deal. We asked them to give us three months to make some improvements and if after three months they didn't think that anything had changed that we would let them go and wish them well guilt free.

The First Sergeant and I decided to attack our problem by bringing fun back into drill. Everything that we taught, everything that we trained, every mission that we accomplished would have elements of fun accompanied with mission focused training. We allowed NCOs and Soldiers to create training events and required them to make them entertaining. They were forced to interact with one another, develop creative ways to teach monotonous training, compete with one another on some tasks, and build teams for other tasks. We set goals for the weekend for what we wanted to accomplish and when the training and work were done they were done too. They were released for the day, but we always had something planned for the evening if they wanted to stick around and participate. We adopted the philosophy of work hard, play hard.

At first, there were very few people who hung around for after drill events but eventually, as they grew as a team, the participation after drill increased as well.

During the first six months of our command the First Sergeant and I had addressed all of the issues that they brought up during our initial meeting. They understood the purpose of the Company and how each job played a key role in the company as well as in the battalion and the brigade. They learned how to work together to accomplish their mission. They learned how being a part of a team was not only productive, but when done correctly it was fun. They learned how to count on one another and how to lean on each other.

As time passed and improvements were made, they learned that they could trust us with their concerns. They learned that we would address their issues and provide solutions or at least an explanation for why something was the way that it was. They discovered that they didn't have to learn from a manual or in a classroom. We empowered them to come up with interesting, fun classes that taught the information without putting the audience to sleep. Obstacle courses, training events with paint ball guns, competition amongst the unit or against other companies, were all fair game.

I remember at one point, members of another unit began inquiring about how to join our unit. Now, our Soldiers weren't only staying but they were referring friends to join us. That was when we knew we were doing something right because just months before members of our unit wanted to leave the unit. I remember specifically two sisters that were in opposing units. The older sister was often annoyed by the fact that our unit was not only having more fun but being released earlier than hers, when the work was done. Our Soldiers were always kind enough to wave at the other unit as they departed for the American Legion.

We held "sensing" meetings about twice a year during our command and learned something new every time we held one. During the last one we held the Soldiers struggled to come up with things to fix. The list of things that they liked about the unit far outweighed the things they didn't like. After our last session I remember the First Sergeant saying to me:

Well Ma'am I think we did it. We managed to get through two years of command without doing any "Army" training.

What he meant was we accomplished the tasks and the training that was required by the Army, but we did it in a way that didn't feel like work; we had fun.

When the First Sergeant and I left command our unit was at 98% strength. We were able to retain the large majority of Soldiers we had and recruit and retain others to remain and join our ranks. We were a solid unit that not only worked together to form a team but grew leaders along the way. Several of those Soldiers who were "definitely" getting out of the military once their contract was up went on to attend Officer Candidate School or gain full time employment with the National Guard. Many of the Soldiers from that unit have joined the Facebook page I created and are sharing their positive memories of the time we spent together. Empowering and educating people in your organization are great tools toward success.

Step 4 — Empower and Educate (continued)

All of your team members have ideas, thoughts, and opinions, and when they aren't able to voice them they feel insignificant. There is an apathy that develops when they don't feel they are part of the plan, and apathy can go viral within your team if you don't allow them to have a voice. It is very easy to implement a program that allows them to voice their opinion. All you have to do is ask them for input, and they will provide it. Although this is easy to accomplish, it will take time for the team to trust you enough to feel comfortable sharing their thoughts and opinions. This is why Step 1 – Develop Relationships—is so important to achieve first. After accomplishing Step 1, the other steps are easier to achieve. You have to prove that you care enough to listen, that you heard them, and that you implemented or fixed what they shared. It isn't enough to ask and never do anything with the information.

回回

H I N T :
You have to show them that you heard them and that you care and then use part or all of their ideas or be prepared to tell them why you didn't.

回回

If the information that they shared is an issue that needs to be addressed you must fix the problem or a portion of the problem and let them know how you fixed it. This process shows them their concerns and ideas are not falling on deaf ears and they can trust you with their concerns. After you have established you are listening and you care about them then they will begin to believe their opinion matters and that they are, in fact, part of a team, not a dictatorship.

This can be accomplished by holding a "sensing session" or a "town hall meeting" similar to the one that my First Sergeant and I held with our company. You can call it whatever you want as long as the intent is communicated to the audience. It is important that every member of the team is present for the meeting. You should identify the purpose of the meeting, assign a facilitator, establish ground rules for contribution, and assign a scribe to capture the comments during the meeting. I know that this may seem very structured, but these components are necessary for a successful meeting of this kind. If not structured and facilitated, it could turn into a blood bath quickly, and that could be disastrous to the team. Here is an example of what a sensing session might look like and how to communicate your vision/goals for the session.

- **Purpose:** Ensure that the purpose is clearly stated. For example, to discuss issues and concerns related to work place policy and procedures in order to improve our work environment, become a more effective and efficient team, and enhance team morale.

- **Assign a Facilitator:** Ideally, this should be you or your "second" in charge, someone that is capable and authorized to make decisions for the team. During the session there will be issues and concerns that come up that have already been recognized or addressed or have been noticed and are currently being addressed. The facilitator must be "in the know" about the current state of the team and the organization so they can address these comments and provide a response to concerns that have been recognized prior to the session. As the Team Leader, acting as the facilitator gives you the opportunity to address all of the concerns personally as well as provide background information on issues they may not be informed about. Additionally, acting as the facilitator will establish credibility for you as their leader. If another person acts as the facilitator he appears to be the subject matter expert and that may lead to respect and credibility issues for you.

- **Ground Rules:** This is not a "bitch" session. Allow others to express their concerns and be respectful of each other. Do not talk over one another; allow team members to complete their comments before you speak. Speak the truth. There will be no repercussions on opinions and suggestions offered. The meeting will be an hour, notes will be taken and distributed to attendees or their supervisors, and updates will be distributed.

- **Capture Comments:** Assign someone to not only take notes but write the comments or concerns in a place that can be seen during the meeting.

回 凹

H I N T :
Make notes visible by using hard copy written on pages, a white board, or project notes typed on the computer during the meeting. The notes need to be visible to the team. This allows the team members to know that their comments have been captured and heard.

回 凹

This person will also transcribe the notes and send a copy to the participants, again as proof that their comments have been captured.

This format, when facilitated properly, is successful, productive, organized, and respectful. A large amount of information can be gained in a short amount of time, and team members will feel heard, respected, and empowered.

Some organizations or teams use a suggestion box as a means to gain information and suggestions for improvement. Personally, I don't like the suggestion box method because it doesn't allow for elaboration on the issue, and it doesn't require face to face communication. If you have developed relationships with your team they should be comfortable coming to you about any issue. Instead of clearly expressing concerns and addressing them rationally, team members are allowed to hide their feelings behind anonymity with a suggestion box. When issues are discussed in an open forum you can get a feel for if it is a team issue or an individual issue, which may change how the issue is addressed. In addition, when done publicly, solutions are often arrived at on the spot, instead of waiting for someone to actually look in the suggestion box to find your concern.

It's also worth mentioning that when teams discuss problems together and solve problems together they become a stronger team.

回 凹

H I N T :
Very seldom is anonymity the best method for bringing problems to the table. There are, however, instances related to conduct where anonymity is the best course of action; as a general rule I wouldn't suggest this method.

回 凹

They Matter to the Success of the Team

I used to be in charge of a mentoring program for 16 to 18 year old at risk youth. As part of the program, we would match the youth with a mentor who would assist him or her during the resident program as well as during the non-resident phase of the program. We provided both the mentee and the mentor with training to ensure they understood their responsibilities to the relationship. We spent eight hours with them preparing them for situations they might encounter during the relationship; we instructed them on how to complete required reports; and finally we allowed them time to spend with each other. At the end of each training session we conducted a ceremony solidifying the relationship and the commitment they had made to one another. During that ceremony we presented them with a certificate and a *Starfish* pin. The author of the starfish story is unknown but it is represented below.

> *One day an older man was walking down the beach when he saw a young boy picking up starfish and hurling them into the ocean. The old man approached the boy and asked, "Young man, can I ask what you are doing?" The boy replied, "I'm throwing the starfish back into the ocean before the sun kills them." The old man shook his head and scoffed at the boy and said, "Son, there are thousands of miles of beach and hundreds of starfish. It won't matter how many you throw back in, more will wash ashore." The boy looked at the old man and contemplated what he had just said, and then he reached down picked up another starfish while staring at the old man, threw it back into the ocean, and said "It mattered to that one."*

Never underestimate the power that your words and actions have or the impact that you can have on one person.

It's critical that each team member understands that his effort, knowledge, and experience are crucial to the success of the team. Insure they all know how they are contributing. This is what I call the "big picture" speech. As I stated in Step 1, it's vital that each team member understands how their piece affects the whole of the team and the organization. This step goes hand in hand with the earlier approach, "let them be heard." If they know their opinions matter and that you value their input then they will feel empowered to provide it more often.

回 리

H I N T :

Asking for feedback and opinions does not make you incompetent, insecure, weak, or intellectually inferior. Asking for feedback and opinions is the sign of a good leader who cares about the success of the team. Do not let anyone tell you any different. Odds are the person who says those things has an ineffective, disgruntled team whose creativity is stifled by their leader.

回 리

CHAPTER 12

Well done is better than well said..

~ **Benjamin Franklin**, One of the Founding Fathers of the
United States of America ~

回 回

TRUST THEM WITH SOMETHING IMPORTANT!

At one point in my career a staff member told me: "I'm always happy to see you. Because no matter how messed up things are, I know that when you get here you will fix them, and I know if things aren't messed up, you'll make them even better."

As flattering as those words were, I realized that at some level I had failed as a leader. If I had to arrive to "fix" things or make them "even better" then I had not properly trained or empowered my subordinates to take appropriate actions in my absence. A tell-tale sign of a good leader is an organization that runs smooth in that leader's absence.

Step 4 — Empower and Educate (*continued*)

At a certain point in every relationship with a team member you will realize he is ready for more responsibility. You will have team members that crave additional tasks in order to grow and progress throughout the organization. You will have team members that need additional responsibility to give them purpose and significance. It's important, however, to know that additional responsibility isn't always what your team member wants. You will also have team members that shy away from additional responsibility due to stress, fear, or apathy. In some cases you may have to push additional responsibility on team members even if they aren't ready. This normally happens when the requirements placed on the team exceed the people trained to accomplish the goals. This will be addressed later during the education portion of this chapter. For now let us assume that you have team members that are ready and able to take on additional responsibility. Again, knowing your team will help you identify who is who and how best they can help the organization.

Regardless of the makeup of your team, because you will more than likely have all of the team members I just described, you need to showcase them.

CAUTION:
Some team members will claim that they don't want the attention, but I would submit to you that most people want to be noticed. Not all publicly, but noticed none the less.

Showing faith in them and their skills and giving them *important* tasks shows that you trust them to accomplish the task. Your words should tell them that you recognize their skills, trust that they can accomplish the task, and are counting on them to prevail. You should also convey to them that you and the rest of the team are there to support them if and when they need guidance and assistance. Constantly reinforcing your support and faith in them and the support of the team breeds confidence and reduces fear when team members are faced with difficult tasks. This will empower them to succeed or identify for you that they need additional coaching or training. I want to highlight IMPORTANT task because if the task has little or no significance then the completion of the task and the feelings of trust and empowerment will not be felt by the team member. A less important task is simply that, just another task.

Benjamin Franklin's quotation, "Well done is better than well said," at the beginning of this chapter speaks volumes. It could be taken several ways, but I prefer to think of it in the context of doing something is much more satisfying than talking about doing something. It's great to be a part of a team that accomplished a task but even better to be the person that was in charge of the team that accomplished the task. Let's face it, that's why you're reading this book; you are a leader or you want to become one.

Allow them to make decisions without you

You are going to have team member's at all different levels of knowledge, skill, and experience. Team members will learn and grow at different paces, and they all won't be ready for the "important" task. However, all team members need to feel that they are empowered, only if a little. If you have team members that aren't ready to be assigned to important tasks but you still want to empower them, give them the authority to make certain decisions without your input or approval. Each team member should be in charge of her own "domain." There are certain things that they will do on a daily basis that are essential to the team, and only they do them. Regardless of the importance or the critical nature of the task, it's theirs! Give them the authority to make decisions about those things, and allow them to "own" the process, the product, and the decision.

CAUTION:
Requiring team members to constantly gain your approval, with regard to decisions, where they are more knowledgeable than you can be demeaning.

Giving them the authority to make small decisions provides them a sense of significance for that particular task. Let them know that you trust them to make those decisions, and they are immediately empowered and feel valued. Because let's face it, they probably know more about it than you do.

These decisions don't have to be big decisions. They can be as simple as the following:

- Ordering office supplies
- Sending a report to your boss
- Managing your daily calendar
- Maintaining office equipment
- Monitoring compliance rosters

These are just some examples to help you understand, but there are many more that I'm sure you can think of on your own. If you are already doing this with some of your team members, just make sure they know they own the task and you trust them to complete it without you.

CHAPTER 13:

Before everything else, getting ready is the
secret of success.

~ **Henry Ford**, American industrialist ~

回回

TELL THEM THEY
ARE NEXT

Do you remember as a kid always wanting to be older so you could do the things that older kids were doing?

> **Child:** "Why do I have to go to bed but Amy gets to stay up?"
> **Mother:** "Because your sister is older. When you get older you can stay up later too."

I always cringed when I heard "the age" justification. Although it was better than the alternative of "because I'm your mother and I said so, that's all the 'why' you need" justification, it was still not preferred. However, as an adult this tactic totally makes sense to me now. Then I was given a brief glimpse of

what life was going to be in the future, and that modified my
behavior in the present.

- If you clean your room, you can go play.
- Eat your vegetables and you can have dessert.
- If you get good grades, you can use the car.

No kid wants to clean his room, eat her vegetables, or
study, but providing a reward makes it all worth it.

In the case of hard working employees, they are going to
continue to perform for you but when they know they are next
it makes the hard work an easier pill to swallow. Show them
what they have to look forward to and tell them they are next.

Step 4 — Empower and Educate (continued)

It's been my experience that no matter how balanced your team
is there are always "rock stars" that stand out above the rest.
These team members are the ones that have vision, can accomplish a task with little guidance or supervision, and are the
ones that will eventually have your job. These team members
are the ones you count on when you are in a crunch situation
and need a project completed quickly. They are the ones you
trust. They are the ones that you would not hesitate leaving in
charge in your absence. They are the team members you assign
important tasks. They put in extra time, continually trying to
improve themselves and the team. They assist others on the
team to learn and grow, and they are always looking to challenge themselves. They get assigned more tasks or responsibility than other team members. They have a strong work ethic
and a desire to learn, grow, and succeed. They are next!

These team members are great to have on your team, but
be careful not to take advantage of their drive and ambition.

Even the most ambitious team members will reduce their performance or worse, leave the organization if they do not feel appreciated or valued. If they know they are next for a promotion or a position and you are grooming and mentoring them for a future assignment they have a goal to work toward. They know you have recognized their potential and are actively managing their career and their efforts will eventually be rewarded. If, on the other hand you don't acknowledge their efforts and inform them of your plans for their future, or worse you don't have plans for their future, then you could lose them to another organization.

回凹

HINT:
Telling team members they are next empowers and motivates them to continue to grow and achieve and ultimately brings great success to the team.

回凹

Additionally, don't make your plans for them a secret to the rest of the team. Acknowledging a strong team member creates a healthy competition and allows others to see what characteristics or skills are needed to succeed. This also provides them with additional support when you aren't available. If the team knows "who is next" they will utilize that person's knowledge and experience to guide them in your absence.

CHAPTER 14:

Life is often compared to a marathon, but
I think it is more like being a sprinter; long
stretches of hard work punctuated by brief
moments in which we are given the opportunity
to perform at our best.

~ **Michael Johnson**, Olympic Gold Medalist ~

回 回

BEST IN SHOW

The concept of "Best in Show" simply means to give kudos and
accolades to those that deserve it, publicly, to your supervisors.
Showcase and brag about your staff to your boss. When I was
younger I didn't understand the importance of the "Best in
Show" principle. I was inexperienced, anxious, and uncomfort-
able when my supervisors were around and honestly couldn't
wait for them to leave. So the last thing I wanted to do was to
prolong their stay by introducing them to a bunch of people.

I learned the importance of this principle on a hot day in
July in Wisconsin. I was a Company Commander and for some
reason during a field training exercise a General Officer came
to our area of operation. As the senior officer in the Company

I was responsible for escorting the General around our area and briefing him on our mission. As I walked around to each section within the company I briefly described the purpose of the section and any ongoing missions.

At one point in the briefing one of my Lieutenants joined the tour and remained with us until the General's departure. This particular Lieutenant was responsible for a large operation during this training cycle and was in charge of a very highly visible operation that was a key component of many units arriving at the training. He and his section had performed their duties flawlessly and although I had given them kudos for doing so, I didn't take the opportunity to showcase him or his section when I had the opportunity. I remember the Lieutenant's words and more specifically his look of disgust and disappointment in me after the General left. "Thanks for introducing me to the General, Ma'am." He said it with a touch of disrespect as he turned and walked back to his area, but I deserved it! He was right to say something and from that point forward I never made that mistake again.

Step 4 — Empower and Educate (*continued*)

Once your team members reach a point when they can be trusted with important tasks, know they are next and you allow them to make decisions in your absence; show them off. Allow them to create and brief proposals, ask them to represent you and the team in a high level meeting with your superiors, give them credit for projects that they had a significant contribution in and allow them to be seen by YOUR supervisors. Showcase their talent in front of their peers and their hierarchy. Ask them to provide a training session for the team or give an update on a project. There are many ways to put them in front of the crowd and showcase their talent. Providing them this kind of exposure exhibits confidence in their skills and rewards their efforts.

When providing them with this type of opportunity, it's essential that you prepare them. It is your responsibility to ensure that they are prepared for the briefing, proposal, meeting, or training. By putting them up front you are announcing to the community that you have faith in the individual's ability to handle the situation. If they fail, it's a direct reflection on you. Review their proposal or training, require them to brief you or one of their superiors prior to the real briefing, provide guidance and training, and edit all products before distribution.

Know that even with proper preparation, they won't get it right every time, but this is just an opportunity to mentor and coach them on areas that need improvement.

Also, inform your supervisors that you are giving the team member this opportunity. Don't surprise them by having a subordinate show up in your absence; that will normally upset your boss and not be a good experience for your team member.

回 凹

HINT:
The best approach to showcasing your team member is to put him out front but be there in the background to assist and support in the event he is not able to answer a question or needs your support. This still puts him in the spot light but provides a security blanket to reduce his stress and nerves. Eventually, he will be able to do it on his own.

回 凹

The previous chapters have given you some ideas about ways to empower your team. Anything that you can do to make your team part of the decision making process will show them their opinion matters, their efforts are recognized, and that you have confidence in them. All of these things will lead your team members to work effectively and efficiently for you, the team, and the organization.

CHAPTER 15:

If someone is going down the wrong road, he doesn't need motivation to speed him up. What he needs is education to turn him around.

~ **Jim Rohn**, entrepreneur, author and motivational speaker ~

回回

TRAIN, MENTOR, COACH AND DEVELOP

Train, mentor, coach and develop; my absolute favorite thing to do! Once you have mastered Steps 1 and 2 people will flock to you to gain nuggets of information and guidance that can be provided in Step 4. Theodore Roosevelt said it best: "Nobody cares how much you know, until they know how much you care." Once they know that you care, they will seek you out for mentorship and coaching.

In the meantime, it's your responsibility to use every opportunity that you have to train, mentor, coach, and develop your team.

Step 4 – Empower and Educate (*continued*)

Educate them

Once you truly become a leader, you stop being your number one priority. It is your responsibility to train, mentor, coach, and develop your team. You should have a team mindset and continue to promote and educate them along the way to ensure that the team and the organizational goals are met. Your individual goals take a back seat to the goals and accomplishments of your team. Your concentration should be on developing them into better employees and team members.

◙◙

H I N T :
Your goals are achieved when the team
succeeds not the other way around.

◙◙

In order for any team to grow and continue to achieve and set higher standards and goals, they need knowledge. From the newest member of the team to the wily veteran, continually learning means continual growth. It doesn't matter how old they are, how long they have been with the team, or how many degrees they have; continued education is essential to personal growth as well as to the growth of the team.

Learning is not reserved for your team members. You as their leader are responsible for continuing your education as well. It is essential for you to constantly learn and improve your skills just as you will require of your team. In order to be an effective leader you need to keep up with new technologies, methods, products, and advances in your field. You need to be looking toward the future at all times, or one day you will look ahead and see the back of your competitors head. As they race forward increasing their performance and maintaining relevance in the marketplace, you continue to use antiquated techniques, disappoint your customer, and reduce your profit share. It's not always easy to keep up with the latest and greatest, but luckily you don't have to do it on your own. You do, however, have to provide opportunities to your team to assist you with the task. In the chapters that follow I will share with you several training methods that will insure your team is trained to the level necessary for success, individually and organizationally.

As I refer to these training methods I would like you to remember two things; training should always be relevant, and you should make every effort to make it fun! Training will be discussed later in the Communication portion of the Approach, but I feel it is important to mention it here so you do not lose sight of it during education.

Train for Effect not Activity

When you require your team to participate in training, make it mean something. Insure the training allows them to learn, develop, grow, or progress. The last thing a team member wants to do is to spend three days in a "training" seminar and learn nothing. When asked what they learned their response is "nothing, it was a complete waste of time." We have all attended training like that and all wished that we could get those three days back to do something productive. Ensure the training they are receiving is worthwhile, not only for them but for the team.

◧◨

H I N T :
Effective training acts as a motivator, and
often times the break from the office is
just what was needed to energize a team
member into action.

◧◨

Unfortunately, it can be difficult to make some training entertaining and effective. Yearly training requirements that every organization mandates can be difficult to pep up, but for the training you have control over, make it worth their while.

Keep in mind that training doesn't have to be associated to your company or your organization in order for it to be considered relevant. There are plenty of opportunities for training that have nothing to do with your service or your product but they have much to do with providing a valuable education to your team.

As a leader, you need to be on the lookout for education that will strengthen the individuals on your team, ultimately making the team stronger.

◧◨

H I N T :
It is much easier to get training approved
if you can show your hierarchy how it
will benefit the organization.

◧◨

Individual and Organizational Training

Always encourage your team to pursue higher education, whether higher education is an Associate's Degree, a Master's Degree, a certification, or an educational opportunity within the company. Keep them learning and engaged and encourage them to grow.

Ensure that you keep accurate and up to date training files on all team members. These records will assist you with evaluations as well as compliance requirements. Compliance requirements are normally mandatory training events necessary for maintaining employment with an organization. Some common compliance training may include:

- Sexual Harassment Training
- Computer Management
- Information Assurance
- Diversity Training
- Suicide Prevention
- Safety
- Emergency Management Procedures

Ensure that each team member, upon completion of training, especially compliance training, is presented with a certificate of completion and that the certificate is placed in their file for future reference. If training is worth attending, it is worth issuing a training certificate or at the very least a letter from you stating that the member completed the training.

These certificates are not just for compliance but also for justification of completion. Team members may be able to use the completion certificate when applying for other positions or as proof that they have achieved the proper education level in order to be promoted or given a bonus.

In addition to compliance training there are several professional development opportunities that you can offer your team members that will improve the organization as well as their personal growth. Some of these may include:

- Leadership Development
- Time Management
- Conflict Resolution
- Critical Thinking Skills
- Computer Systems Training
- Customer Service Training
- Public Speaking Training
- Sales Training
- Management Skills
- Effective Communication
- Career Management

All of these educational opportunities provide training that will allow the individual and the organization to grow. Do not be stingy in allowing them to attend; they will pay off in the end.

Most of the training can be completed "in house" at little cost to the organization. As their leader, you should be able to teach most of these topics with ease. If you are not currently at that level, you need to get there soon. As I stated earlier, training and education are not just for your team. You have to educate yourself so you can train your team.

There is, however, training that you cannot do yourself. My recommendation is to do as much as you can with the assets that you have. Again, do not sacrifice the quality of training but make an effort to hold the training yourself. Some of the advantages to conducting your own training include:

- Control over content and time
- Control of the quality of trainers

- Shared experience with team
- Development of team members assisting with the training
- Reduced cost

If the budget permits, you may have funding to bring in outside trainers. If possible research the course objectives and the quality of the course prior to sending a large number of people. As I stated earlier, do not train for activity or just to check a box. Ensure the training is worthwhile and not a waste of time for your staff.

Discuss a discounted rate for continued business or large numbers of attendees with the sales person to receive the best price. Shop around for the training program that best fits your needs and the needs of your team, but don't sacrifice the quality of the training to accommodate your budget. If you have a large enough number of participants the trainer will normally come to you and conduct the training in your facility. This may cost a little more but it will save you the cost of sending a large number of team members to another location. In house training saves you travel, lodging, and meal costs as well as additional days lost due to travel. Weigh your options prior to deciding on your method of training.

CAUTION:
Don't pay top dollar for a training program where the training is delivered right to the team member's desk. There are too many distractions in that cubicle and the surrounding area, and you will not get your money's worth, regardless of how good the training is. If there is a webinar or teleseminar training that you want your team to attend, hold it in a separate location in the office, away from their desks and other distractions.

Education is essential to every team's growth. Make sure the education is worth the investment.

Some organizations have a required education program built into them and will have expectations that their employees achieve certain levels of education. If this is the case with your organization, make it very clear to them what is expected and when it is expected to be completed.

CHAPTER 16:

Try not to become a man of success. Rather
become a man of value..

~ **Albert Einstein**, theoretical physicist ~

回 回

GIVE THEM THE TOOLS FOR SUCCESS

Step 4 — Empower and Educate (continued)

Training does not have to be an organized, sit down, planned event. The opportunities to train your team are vast. They can happen during a short conversation, while doling out tasks and guidance, while listening to a webinar, following a mistake, or any number of other times during the course of the day. We are constantly learning and growing and should never miss an opportunity to allow our team to drink from our fountain of knowledge.

Honestly, our actions and reactions can be some of the best lessons. My high school English teacher, Mrs. Slack, was a great example of this. She was stern and a little grumpy. She was fair and often times funny but always a professional. You always knew where you stood with her, and you always knew that she was in charge of the classroom. She didn't accept excuses and loathed whiners but was respectful of her students and the process of education. Her actions and reactions probably taught me more than the lesson plans and the curriculum. She was one of the most respected teachers in our school, and she taught me much more than English.

Values

One of the most important pieces of knowledge that you can provide your team is the knowledge of what you, their boss, values. If this is not communicated to them they will spend unnecessary time on things that hold less importance for you and the organization. This is precious time that could be used more effectively on the right things. You have to tell them what is important to you, the organization, and the team. Values are those things that have personal or organizational worth or meaning. These are not just a list of politically correct terms that organizations throw out in a mission statement or a vision statement.

Values convey to the public and to the organization's employees what is important to you and therefore what should be important to them. As a leader, your values need to be aligned with the organizational values; they need to be a culture that is present throughout the organization. You can add to the organizational values but you cannot take away from them. In other words, you may want to add additional personal or professional values to what the organization has already communicated, but you cannot delete from their values.

As I said, the organizational values are organization wide and run throughout. They are the values that the founders believed to be imperative when building the company and are therefore constant values throughout all divisions, departments, and teams within the company.

It is essential that these values and your values are communicated to your team during the initial counseling. These values set the stage for the culture of the organization and act as a report card for all things within the culture.

Resources

There are some basics that every team member should be provided in order to have a clear picture of the organization, their values, and the resources available to them.

- Organizational structure
- Leadership philosophy
- Company/team vision and mission
- Historical data
- Manuals
- Policies and procedures
- Contact information
- Share drive access
- Duties and responsibilities

These are all great tools for your team members. These tools provide them with what they need to achieve the results you expect from them. However, don't assume that they know where to find them or that they even know to look for them. It's your responsibility to ensure they have access to these things and that they know where to get them.

These tools should be readily accessible to every team member and should be presented to them early on in the orientation process. They can be disseminated during the company orientation, if you have one, but make sure they are explained and not just handed to them. Too often organizations hold ineffective orientations for new employees. Orientations should be well organized, short briefings that provide valuable information for the employee.

CAUTION:

Orientations should not be one person standing in the front of the room droning on about policy and procedure, resulting in the employee walking away with an armful of information that will probably never be looked at again.

Although orientations are sometimes necessary to accomplish required paperwork for employment it isn't necessary to inundate employees with boring policy and procedure. Orientation time would be better spent introducing the new team member to their new team and the office surroundings. As we discussed in Chapter 2, a sponsor or another team member can be a great bridge for the new team member. Assigning a sponsor creates an immediate ally for the new team member and gives him access to someone who knows the ropes, can introduce him to key players, and can answer questions.

CAUTION!

Pick a sponsor that is friendly, knowledgeable, and willing to take on the role. Do not assign someone to be a sponsor if you wouldn't want her as YOUR sponsor!

The tools listed above should be provided to the new team member during the orientation, by the sponsor, during the initial counseling, or a combination of all three.

As I stated earlier, training comes in all shapes and sizes. At a minimum there should be a core set of training that every team member receives in order for there to be a consistent foundation for all. Then, depending on the position or task team members are being asked to perform, additional training should be provided.

As an example, the United States Army trains every Soldier Infantry skills during basic training. Everyone is not going to become an Infantry Soldier; however, those are the skills that every Soldier receives as he or she enters the Army. They are necessary skills that provide the foundation for every Soldier and are therefore known by all. After basic training, Soldiers go to their Advanced Individual Training (AIT) where they receive additional training based on their Military Occupational Specialty (MOS). It is specific to them and the job that they are going to perform in the Army. As they go through their career they will be required to attend additional training based on assignments and the needs of the Army.

If a Soldier comes to a unit as a trained mechanic and the unit Commander needs that Soldier to be a Retention Specialist, the Commander will send that Soldier to a school that teaches him how to be a Retention Specialist. The Commander couldn't give him an additional duty and expect him to be successful without providing the training to be successful. Similarly, you wouldn't give a team member a task to accomplish and expect her to be successful without providing the appropriate training necessary to perform the task. Of course, you could give her a task without training, but what product would you receive in turn? Trust me, the time and the money are worth it to get a good product when you need it.

Many leaders use the excuse of not having the time or money, but there is always a way and great leaders always find it. Resources are often excuses for "why not," but resourcefulness trumps the lack of resources every time.

回口

H I N T :
**If you are managing them properly, they
will have completed the training before
you need them to perform the task.**

回口

CHAPTER 17

I tried daydreaming once, but my mind
kept wandering.

~ **Steven Wright**, Comedian ~

回回

CAN YOU HEAR ME NOW?

Have you ever known anyone who you wish you could just "turn off?" Someone so annoying you wished that you had a mute button? When I was a kid, I remember going to my grandparents' house and experiencing this very phenomenon. My Grandpa wore hearing aids and as he would sit in the living room watching whatever western was on TV, he would hear just fine. Oddly enough, though, the sound of my Grandma's voice was rarely audible to him, after he turned his hearing aid down that is. You could hear her three houses down the block, but Grandpa would sit in his chair and be oblivious to the high pitched "HAAAAAAARRRRROOOOOOLLLLLLLLD!"

My Grandpa's name was Harold, and my grandma could turn that two syllable name into a 30 second screech that would raise the hair on the back of your neck. It started off slowly with a couple of "Harold's" and then increasingly became louder and longer. By about the fourth or fifth attempt you knew it would be followed by her standing in direct line of sight of the TV and demanding "Harold, turn your hearing aid back on; I know you heard me the first time." He would begrudgingly comply, and at that point communication could begin.

Step 5 — Communication and Counseling

Communication is a fairly simple design that consists of three elements, in my opinion. The sender sends a message, the receiver receives the message, and feedback is exchanged. Part of the sender's job is to encode the message so it can be understood by the receiver and in turn it is the receiver's job to decode the sender's message. It seems like a very simple process, yet we screw it up all the time.

Communication has been a mystery for many years and is not exclusive to the work place. Communication gaps have been present for years in marriage, parent/child relationships, friendships, and the work place. Communication is vital to everything we do and conversely the scapegoat for most things that we do not do. I could write an entire book just on effective communication, but others have already done that so I'm going to concentrate on the basics with regard to building your team.

Due to the nature of this book, I have already discussed quite a bit about communication as it relates to developing relationships, inspiring, empowering, and rewarding team members. I will not go through those topics again but keep in mind that just because they are not in the communication section does not mean that they are not essential to effective communication.

Training should be Entertaining

According to Carver, Johnson, & Friedman (1970) the average human only speaks at a rate of 125 words per minute during an ordinary conversation, and a speaker in front of an audience slows down to around 100 words per minute? Any idea how fast listeners listen? An audience will listen or think as they listen between 400 and 500 words per minute. What does that tell you? It should tell you that whenever you are providing training you need to insure that the audience is stimulated, otherwise they will use those other 400 words to listen or think about something other than you!

Let me share with you a little secret: For most of your team work is not their number one priority. Shocking? Not so much. Spouse, kids, family, pets, to do lists, house cleaning, soccer practice, church, volunteer work, vacation, appointments, illnesses, and finances are just a few of the things that are on their minds during the work day. So, if you create training events that are boring, uninformative, and a waste of time they are going to be thinking and listening to themselves and not to the trainer.

回回

H I N T :
Putting together a training event for adults is similar to hosting a birthday party for children. You want to ensure that there are several different forms of activities and stimulation to keep their attention.

回回

There are three types of learners outlined in Terry Farwell's article *Visual, Auditory, Kinesthetic Learners* on www.school.familyeducation.com: auditory, those that learn by hearing; visual, those that learn by seeing something in action; and kinesthetic, those that learn by doing. Rarely will you find an individual that responds, strictly, to one type of learning. Although a person may be partial to a particular type of learning, normally what you will discover is that a combination of different learning types provides the highest amount of comprehension of the task at hand. That being said, you want to insure that your training has elements of all three types of learning. This will ensure that all of your trainee's learning styles are met.

Also, when creating a training event for your team, make sure they are professionally designed as if you were performing the training in front of your boss. Do not take short cuts on presentation materials, trainers, snacks, or event locations. Set the standard of excellence to create a comfortable, worthwhile, professional, learning experience.

This is really very simple to do and when accomplished produces a high energy, fast moving, entertaining, professional atmosphere for your participants. Below are some tips on creating a productive, informative, fun training event that will entice your audience.

✔ Do not attempt to perform all training within your team by yourself. First of all it adds undue stress to design, organize, and implement the entire training program. Second, as mentioned earlier in the chapter, putting people out front provides an opportunity for the team member to excel and succeed. Third, by doing all the training yourself you miss a huge opportunity to develop future leaders. Fourth, by dividing up responsibilities for the training event it becomes a team project and when completed becomes a team success. Lastly, your team will probably get tired of listening to you, regardless of how charismatic you are. If, in the interim of training team members to assist in training, you need assistance with the training ask your peers to assist.

✔ Create your agenda and dole out trainer assignments as soon as possible to give your trainers time to prepare, review, and rehearse their training. Provide clear guidance as to the content you want them to train and set deadlines for the task completion dates.

✔ Hand pick your speakers/trainers. If they can't perform to the standard you want, don't ask them to be trainers. Often leaders will select trainers based on knowledge and disregard performance ability altogether; this is a huge mistake! Either learn the material yourself or coach them on their presentation skills, but don't put a boring, monotone trainer in front of your team!

囗囗

H I N T :
The smartest trainer in the world will fail to educate if he can't connect with the audience.

囗囗

✔ Review all presentations for accurateness and content and rehearse with presenters whenever possible prior to training. This is your training event, insure that everything is in it that you want trained and that the product is as close to error free as possible. People can be critical, catty, and judgmental; don't give them any reason to discount the training product.

✔ Create an agenda that is 60 percent "in motion" and 40 percent "at rest." If you design an agenda that is filled with Power Point presentations you will lull the audience to sleep or at the very least give them an excuse to use their smart phone for entertainment.

A training event needs to have all of the learning styles woven into it (auditory, visual, and kinesthetic). Power Point is visual and the presentation of the slides is auditory but it is not kinesthetic. You need to be able to introduce all forms of learning throughout the course of the training event in order to ensure you are reaching all learning styles and keeping the attention of your audience. Use the following to break up your training event into effective training blocks that will keep the attention of the audience.

- Short video clips
- Live internet page navigation
- Guest speakers via web cameras
- Individual assessment tests or surveys
- Training evaluation reports
- Group brain storming sessions
- Group activities
- Group event broken down by teams
- Activity involving a portion of group
- Skit or role play
- Lecture

These are just some ideas to change up the pace of the training and keep it interesting.

◲ ◱

H I N T :
I once held a training event for my staff
where I provided them each with a buck-

et of Legos and encouraged them to create a masterpiece by the end of the conference that would be judged and awarded a prize. Knowing even then that people can listen faster than I could talk, I gave them something to focus their energy on while they listened. It inspired competition, encouraged creativity, provided a reward, and kept them focused on the topic.

🔲🔲

✔ Prepare the training venue, conference room, or classroom prior to the trainees arriving. You need to arrive well in advance of the participants to ensure everything is in place and ready to go for the event. Some typical obstacles that may occur if not checked ahead of time:

- Burnt out light bulbs in overhead projectors
- Microphones that don't work
- No internet access
- Computer and projector aren't "talking" to one another
- Forgotten dry erase markers, laser pointers, slides, handouts, etc.
- Room too small; room too big

Rehearsing ahead of time, anticipating these issues and others like them, and having back up plans are the best defense against unanticipated venue complications. The worst thing you could do is ignore this preparation stage and risk looking ill prepared and unprofessional in front of your team.

✔ Schedule hourly breaks to allow participants to decompress from learning. Some trainers believe that allowing participants to take breaks as needed without scheduling them is a more effective use of time; I disagree. Scheduled breaks allow you or the next trainer to prepare for the next presentation, give participants time to stretch, network, ask questions, or just visit with their teammates. They allow time to conduct personal business, bathroom breaks, coffee refills, and nicotine fixes. Again, these should be hourly, but try not to keep them in their seat for more than an hour and a half, tops.

✔ Make sure that at the end of the event you allow them an opportunity to provide feedback on the content and quality of the event. This lets them know that you value their opinion and want to improve or sustain based on their comments.

Putting in the effort to create a valuable training event will pay huge dividends in the future and show your team that training and knowledge are something that you value. If designed as above, you can also show your team that training does not have to be dry and boring, and they might just look forward to the experience.

I have mentioned several times that training, no matter how you conduct it, needs to be entertaining and have elements of fun. I'm not suggesting that you have bands and clowns and comedians at your training sessions. I am however suggesting that you insert elements of fun into the training. The best activities are those that involve your entire team, allow them to learn, and allow them to get to know one another better.

Examples of Entertaining Training:

- You and your staff kick off a training session by dressing up in costumes and making complete fools out of yourselves by performing some ridiculously silly skit. Lights, music, props, costumes, scripts – the whole bit. Trust me, it's worth it. This type of entertainment sets the tone and shows them that you are willing to embarrass yourself for their pleasure. Over the years I have participated in skits as Wonder Woman, Daisy Duke, Cheryl Miller, a backup dancer for Men in Black, a Survivor contestant...to name a few. This one takes some time to develop but it's worth the time and effort. And, in case you were wondering, I did dress up as Wonder Woman in front of my boss. Bosses have a sense of humor too; he was Superman.

- Create an event outside of the "classroom" setting, and require teams to work together: scavenger hunts, amazing race type events, geocaching, obstacle courses, or anything team based that incites competition. These types of events build team work and morale. They teach conflict resolution, communication, decision making, leadership development, time management, and so much more, but above all they are fun!

- Use organizational terminology or policies and procedures to develop a "Jeopardy" type game that tests their knowledge of certain subjects.

- Ask team members to bring in pictures of themselves from high school and have a competition to see who can correctly match the picture to the team member.

- Have team members develop creative, theme based "learning stations" about a product or a task and require each team member to train her station. To make it entertaining you might have them dress up as their favorite

'70s TV show character and present the information as the character would during that genre.

- Open up a training event with team members putting on a show using "Rock Band" instruments or singing Karaoke.

Some of these may seem pretty far out there, but I promise you they are worth the time and effort.

There are so many ideas to make training fun, the possibilities are endless. Don't concern yourself with making every aspect of your training entertaining, just enough to loosen up the crowd and not take yourself too seriously. Just one or two of these ideas in a two day training session are sufficient. Your team will talk about it for months. I recently had a conversation with a team member who expressed to me how fun an event was that I hosted in 2005. "I still think about that," he related, "that was a lot of fun." And in the for what it's worth category, that team member was one of my biggest challenges when it came to developing a relationship and getting him to buy into the techniques and philosophies of the *D.I.R.E.C.T* Approach. He's a believer now though!

Remember, people want to be a part of a team that works hard together but also plays hard together. Too much work and not enough play makes for a pretty dull work environment. Much of your time will be spent working hard; reward your hard work with a little fun.

回 凹

H I N T :

Training is a way that you communicate with your team. Communicate to your team that quality, creative, entertaining training is not only possible but it is the standard. A standard that they can expect at every training session that you host! Not just because it is fun but because it will engage them, teach them, and hold their interest. Fun is just an added benefit.

回 凹

CHAPTER 18

Electric communication will never be a substitute
for the face of someone who with their soul
encourages another person to be brave and true.

~ **Charles Dickens**, English Writer ~

◙ ◙

THE NATURE OF
THE BEAST

I would guess that many of you know someone who can give
you "the look" and you immediately know you're in trouble or
someone is disappointed in you. My mother mastered and
quite possibly invented "the look." But my mother is not one
dimensional by any means. She has the look, the tone, the
stance, the vocabulary, and absolutely perfected the guilt trip,
but that's for another story.

My mother could communicate novels without saying a
word or very few and to this day, a certain tone in her voice
flashes me back to my youth. Thankfully it's been a long time
since it was directed at me. I don't remember my mother ever

using the "wait until your father gets home" threat; she scared me enough all on her own. Now, don't get me wrong she certainly wasn't abusive, far from it, but she commanded a respect that was undeniable. She communicated volumes, often without uttering a word! When she did speak, she never raised her voice past the "I'm in charge and you can be replaced" tone that my siblings and I knew very well! Controlled but with attitude, a splash of condescension and a big heaping helping of guilt. A recipe that she had perfected over the years, served frequently to the deserved.

Step 5 – Communicate and Counsel

Communicate

First and foremost you must understand that you are communicating constantly. Even when you are not saying a word, your silence, your posture, your mannerisms, and your affect are communicating. For those of you who have experienced "the look" you knew exactly what I was talking about when describing my mother's look and probably pictured your own mother or father striking the same pose. Those looks communicated many emotions and without the owner muttering a word, you know what they are thinking.

That being said, know that your team sees everything. They see your work ethic; they see how you deal with your supervisors; and they see how you communicate with the team. They know if you are a morning person; they know what time you come in and what time you leave; and they know if you have made a mistake.

回 凹

H I N T :
Always own up to your mistakes, every-
one makes them, and your team will
respect you for doing so.

回 凹

So, be cognizant that you are constantly being watched and observed. I say that to remind you that you set the tone for your team.

- If you are angry, they are on edge,
- If you are grumpy, they won't want to engage you,
- If you are stressed, they are stressed,
- If you are in a good mood, they can be in a good mood.

You need to make every effort to remain calm and in control so you can think clearly and lead your team. They are looking to you to be in charge of yourself and the situation at hand; do not disappoint them.

Much of what we say is not about what we say but how we say it. Be conscience of your tone and your body language when speaking to your team. If you are rude, condescending, and short with them when giving instructions or guidance you are probably going to upset them. Think about how you feel when someone upsets you. Angry, guilty, and defensive are all emotions that come to my mind. Be prepared to deal with these emotions and others if you choose to be rude, condescending and short.

I've learned that people will forget what you said, people will forget what you did, but people will never forget how you made them feel.

~Maya Angelou, American author and poet~

No one wants to be spoken down to or made to feel as though they are holding you up from doing something else. It's ok to be direct when providing guidance, but it's not ok to be rude. You can create a professional, safe work environment where team members enjoy working, without being a jerk. Speak to your team members with respect, and they will reward you by returning the favor. Use words that you would want to hear; please, thank you, and could you do me a favor are affective alternatives to other directive language. The position of a leader is an honor, but I would rather be respected as a person first and for my position second.

回凸

H I N T :
People don't want to dread going to work every day. For most of us, going to a job every day is the nature of the beast if we want to put food on the table and sleep in a bed at night. Creating a work environment that is miserable only makes the beast disgruntled. When the beast is disgruntled productivity suffers and the team fails.

回凸

How we communicate

Face to Face
Whenever possible utilize face to face communication with your team members. With the technology of today it is easy to sit behind your desk and communicate with your staff; resist the urge. Although you would think that technology would make communication easier, in some cases, it is the source that has made it harder. Email, in office chat tools, Skype, text, Facebook, and Twitter pale in comparison to good old fashion face to face communication. Understandably it is not the quickest or the most convenient means of communication today but, it is the most effective. At the very least, pick up the phone and actually talk to someone.

Email
How many times, with regard to a gap in communication, have you said or had said to you "I sent you an email." For the record, an email sent does not equal an email received. The receiver could be out of the office, on vacation, behind on their email, or there could be any number of other reasons they never received your email. If you do not attempt to speak with them face to face or at least call them and talk to them then contact might not be made. You could be waiting for a project to be completed without the team member even knowing she is supposed to be completing a project.

Email is a necessary evil in today's work place and I certainly am not suggesting that we stop using it all together. I'm simply suggesting that we do not use it as our only means of communication.

By all means, do not be the person that forwards every email for action without at least discussing the task, subject, or topic of the email in person. Too many people today use email as a "CYA," and unfortunately many people need to, but that does not mean that you cannot have a conversation about the email that you sent. Better yet, have the conversation first and then follow up with the "CYA" email.

The Meeting about the Meeting

As many of us have experienced, and if you haven't you probably will, some people love to have meetings, and most people hate to go to meetings. People dislike meetings because they are poorly run or do not accomplish anything. Time spent in a meeting is time that they could have spent doing something they believe to be productive.

Unfortunately, meetings, like email are often necessary. However, if they are designed correctly they can be very productive. Here are some tips for an effective meeting.

- One person is in charge of the content and flow of the meeting.
- Go into every meeting with an agenda, and publish it prior to the meeting when possible.
- Provide a single format for all participants to brief the status of a project or task.
- Identify one person to collect and collate the slides being presented prior to the meeting.
- Have an audio/visual technician on site if your meeting requires any technology.
- Clearly articulate the Action, the person in charge of completing the action, and a deadline to complete the action prior to leaving the meeting.
- If you have to "table" an action item, set a time to discuss as soon after the meeting as feasible.

- Identify one person to take notes of the meeting and disseminate them to all participants within 48 hours of the completion of the meeting.
- Make every attempt to keep all meetings to an hour.

Again, there are entire books written on how to conduct an effective meeting, but these tips should get you started in the right direction.

When a team communicates on a regular basis, meetings become less of a bore and more of an update or status of projects. A frequent complaint from team members is "that meeting had nothing to do with me." Although it may not seem important for every member to be at every meeting, it is important to hold weekly meetings with all members present. These meetings serve many purposes for the team as a whole.

Meetings provide a venue for the leader to impart guidance to the entire team. This sharing of information and understanding of tasks ensures that the entire team is aware of all the team's projects. Although they are not all responsible for every task, they can speak intelligently about the task or at a minimum direct people to the team member responsible for it, if asked, thus providing good customer service and functioning as a team should.

回回

H I N T :
When a basketball player has the ball and is dribbling down the court the rest of the team does not go sit on the bench. They are there for support; they are part

**of his success and contribute to the play
and ultimately the win.**

回 回

Status of projects should be briefed by team members at meetings and therefore provide the briefer additional briefing experience. When all team members are required to brief, everyone's knowledge about the team and their teammates is expanded. Briefing the team also makes the team members accountable. They will put more effort into the task if the alternative is looking incompetent in front of you and their teammates. Lastly, meetings that require team members to brief or provide an update offers you a method for evaluating their performance.

The bottom line is meetings can be an effective way to communicate with your team.

CHAPTER 19:

Communicate unto the other person that which
you would want him to communicate unto you
if your positions were reversed.

~ **Aaron Goldman**, Author of Everything I Know about
Marketing I Learned from Google ~

回 回

KNOWLEDGE IS
POWERFUL

Step 5 — Communicate and Counsel (*continued*)

Communicate

Every nugget of knowledge that we gain is powerful.
Continuing to learn and grow is our responsibility as leaders.
We owe it to our team and ourselves to know as much about
our job, craft, trade, or market as we possibly can.
Unfortunately, what some leaders fail to understand is that we
have to share that knowledge with our team. My favorite ways

to communicate information are the morning huddle, the weekly staff meeting (discussed in Chapter 18), and the "after the big kids meeting" meeting. My least favorite ways of communication are email and the drive by, which I will also address in this chapter.

The Morning Huddle

A morning huddle is nothing more than the team coming together in a common area of the office to give a quick update. It is literally a five to ten minute, depending on the size of your team, round robin update from all the key players on your team. This is not a sit down meeting; in fact, no one is allowed to sit.

回 四

H I N T :
Requiring team members to stand during the morning huddle encourages them to be brief and to the point.

回 四

The Morning Huddle entails each member addressing their top priorities for the day and letting you know if they need some of your time during the day. It is quick and effective and allows you to know what they are working on so you can decide if that should be their priority or not. It also allows them to schedule time with you to gain additional guidance needed to complete a task. The Morning Huddle is not difficult, not fancy and most importantly, quick and easy to execute.

The Weekly Meeting

At a minimum you need to bring your team together at least once a week, if not for anything else but to gel as a team. Additionally, though, there are plenty of things that happen during the course of the week that can be difficult to keep track of, and a weekly meeting serves this purpose. Schedule a weekly meeting where you require your team to brief you on the status of projects and where you provide new tasks and guidance. In addition to the benefits that I mentioned in Chapter 18, this meeting will reduce the feeling that you are uninformed or out of touch, hold your team accountable for tasks, and provide an opportunity for the team to connect.

The "After the Big Kids Meeting" Meeting

Inevitably you will be required to attend a meeting hosted by your boss, the big kids meeting. This meeting is going to produce additional tasks and projects that weren't on your radar prior to the meeting. It will be necessary to hold a short meeting with your team to inform them of changes in priorities, new deadlines, and additional tasks or simply good to know information. This meeting can be scheduled, but it does not have to be. The most important thing is to clearly articulate that tasks and projects will come out of this meeting that weren't on the "to do list" before and that they may take priority over something members are currently working on. Again, communicating to them the new task, where it came from, why it's important, and what the new priorities and deadlines are, are keys to effective communication. Remember, purpose, direction, and motivation work much better than "Because I said so."

*You must remain fluid because sometimes
flexible is too ridgid.*

~ Colonel Paul Hastings, U.S. Army ~

Email and The Drive By

Once again, email is not my preferred method of communicating tasks and guidance, but in a pinch I will resort to it. Sometimes you will find yourself alone in the office, after everyone has left for the day, needing to communicate information to your team. When this occurs it always helps to write out an email that clearly articulates guidance to your team. As I stated earlier, it is best to communicate face to face and follow up with an email, but that is not always possible. So, if you do this, tell them it is waiting for them in their inboxes during the morning huddle, and if they have any questions to come see you.

Email is just too impersonal and does not communicate your intent as clearly as face to face communication, no matter how long you make the email.

The drive by is exactly what it sounds like. You are busy moving along in your day on pace with accomplishing what you set out to accomplish and here comes your boss with a drive by task that has to be done before anything else. These types of tasks are just part of the job, but if you are a good leader you will reduce the impact as much as you possible. Take something else off the employee's plate or give him additional help to accomplish the task.

The worst drive by is the one where your boss or another leader from another department tasks your team with something. Again, this is going to happen. The best thing to do in these situations is to make sure that your team comes to you after they receive the task to let you know. You may not always be able to fix this problem, but at least you know that other priorities have taken a back seat to the new ones.

回 凹

H I N T :
It's not your team member's responsibility to argue with other supervisors about tasks. Instruct them to be polite and respectful and to inform you as soon as possible. It is your job to fight those battles not theirs.

回 凹

Regardless of the system used to assign tasks for your team it is important to keep track of all of the tasks in one place. You need to develop an efficient tasking system that specifically communicates the following:

- Outstanding actions
- The person responsible for the action
- The status of the action
- The deadline for completing the action.

This status sheet should be in a public place where all team members can see it or access it, and it needs to be updated regularly. A system like this organizes your projects and makes your staff accountable for their tasks...publicly. Again, this tracking sheet is used as a reference during staff meetings to receive updates on projects. No one wants to be "the guy" that doesn't get his projects done and everyone on the team knows it.

Summary

As you have read in the last couple of chapters, communication is not something that we can avoid nor is it something we should want to avoid. Communication is woven throughout the *D.I.R.E.C.T Approach* and should be used as a tool to develop relationships, inspire, recognize, empower, and counsel. Its presence is necessary for all that we do and accomplish.

I would rather be accused of communicating too much than not enough.

CHAPTER 20:

Effective leadership is putting first things
first. Effective management is discipline,
carrying it out.

~ **Dr. Stephen Covey,** author, The Seven Habits
of Highly Effective People ~

回 回

THE 10 PERCENT

Step 5 — Communicate and Counsel (continued)

Counseling

If you believe counseling is a four letter word, you're doing it
wrong! Counseling is a means to an end. If you want your team
to perform to the best of their ability, to grow, to learn and to
improve then you must counsel them.

Counseling has gotten a bad reputation for years. First,
counseling brings with it a negative connotation. If you are getting counseled, that's bad. Not all counseling has to be bad.
Not to mention, if done right, it is just another conversation
during your day.

Keep in mind that if you have developed a relationship with your team member, provided them purpose, direction and motivation, and rewarded their efforts they are going to want to do right by you and the team. So, the thought of disappointing you should motivate them even more to improve their performance.

I would be lying if I said all counseling is easy; it's just not, but it does not have to be as hard as people make it. Some team members, no matter how hard you try, just don't get it. This could be due to their intelligence, lack of training, apathy, arrogance, or other reasons unknown to you.

> ●◆ When I was a Company Commander my First Sergeant, Earl Mashaw, told me "…you will spend 90% of your time on 10% of the people." Truer words have never been spoken…if you allow it. My suggestion, don't spend your time on the 10%; spend your time on the ones that deserve it and develop them into the next leaders. The 10% will either figure it out, move on or continue to provide you with a challenge. All scenarios increase the effectiveness of the team and/or make you a better leader.

Although some, as I mentioned, are trying and willing they are just not able to give you what you want. Others, however, will challenge you just for sport.

How you deal with this 10% can have a huge effect on the rest of the team. It's important to be mindful of these challenging staff members and not let them get the best of you.

It's important to have a counseling plan that is consistent across the entire team. Just as it is important to have a recognition program in place to reward good behavior, it is equally important to have a discipline program in place to address poor or inadequate behavior. You need to have a clearly defined method that is written, published, and understood by the entire team. It needs to be progressive in nature, consistent, and fair. It may look something like this:

1. Verbal Warning
2. Verbal Counseling
3. Written Counseling #1
4. Written Counseling #2
5. Suspension without Pay
6. Termination

Whatever your discipline program looks like it is up to you to enforce. Keep in mind, though, if you do not do your part to train, mentor, and develop your team, punishing them will be unjust. The onus is on you to prepare them for success.

Types of Counseling

The Initial Counseling
We have already discussed the Initial Counseling in Chapter 2. The purpose of this counseling is to discuss position description, duties, and responsibilities and your expectations for the team member.

Periodic Performance Counseling

This type of counseling should be scheduled regularly throughout the evaluation period. Normally, scheduled quarterly, it is a performance review for the purpose of providing feedback to your team member on his performance. These counseling appointments may seem like an annoyance, but they are crucial to the development of the team member. They allow you to evaluate performance and communicate both positive and negative feedback so the end of year evaluation is not a surprise to the team member. Just as you would not want to wait all year to tell him he is doing a good job, you do not want to wait all year to tell him he is not meeting your expectations. If you wait to tell him, and he has not had time to adjust his performance it is not fair to provide him with a poor evaluation.

Ensure that you are painfully honest during these counseling's. Too often supervisors provide average or above average evaluations to employee's who are not meeting expectations. Employees who receive these evaluations are then confused or frustrated when they are passed up for positions or promotions that they believe they should have received because they think they are on track to advance. Be honest during counseling's and tell your team members where they stand, what their future looks like and what needs to be improved and sustained in order to reach the next level. Do not allow team members to make up their own reasons for why their career isn't progressing! If you leave them to their own imagination they will make their own conclusions and those conclusions rarely reflect the truth.

In some cases this might mean telling a team member that they are not next or that they are not progressing or growing as quickly as you need them to. It may even mean telling them that they should begin looking for another employer. Regardless, you need to tell them the reality of their situation so they can make improvements or begin searching for other employment. Someone once told me, *the certainty of misery is better than the misery of uncertainty.* It might be difficult to hear but telling them their reality, gives them the opportunity to change it!

Behavior Modification Counseling

This counseling is conducted when the team member needs an adjustment to her behavior, attitude, or performance. This counseling is done at the time of, or shortly after, the infraction. Repeated tardiness, missing deadlines, or disrespectful behavior all fall into this category and need to be dealt with sooner than later. Do not wait for the quarterly counseling to address issues that infect the entire team. The rest of your team is looking to you to address and fix these problems. The way you deal with these types of issues will set the tone for the entire team. Discipline and standards provide the framework for all effective teams. When behaviors that effect that discipline and framework are ignored it changes the effectiveness and attitude of the team.

The "Mom" Counseling

Remember when you were younger and you acted out and your Mom would give you the "I'm disappointed in you" speech? I don't know about your Mom but mine never raised her voice while skillfully administering shards of guilt into my psyche. The same concept applies here. When team members become lazy or apathetic or are rushing to accomplish a task and the product is below the standard that you know they are capable of producing, this is a good time for the Mom Counseling. Sometimes team members get in a rut and you need to call them on it and discuss with them the issue.

The "disappointed" speech is also a great tool for the team member that needs a little jolt of reality. This team member is the one that has gotten a little too big for their britches and needs to be brought back down to earth. A reality check or a Mom Counseling will often times do the trick to put that ego in check.

The Play Nice or Move On Counseling

Over the years I have experienced situations where team members have been allowed to simply "exist" in their current position without adding any value to the organization. Once recognized these team members need to be confronted and counseled immediately. These types of team members can be detrimental to your team if they are not held accountable or removed. You can easily spot these team members and so can the rest of your team. These team members normally look like this:

- ✔ Apathetic
- ✔ Bitter and Negative
- ✔ Challenge the hierarchy's decisions
- ✔ Put in the minimum effort required
- ✔ Take every break that is coming to them
- ✔ Provide poor customer service
- ✔ Is against any required training
- ✔ Speaks about retirement often
- ✔ Grumpy and impersonal
- ✔ Opposed to change

These types of employees have never been challenged to do their job and do it well, or they do it well but no one wants to work with them. I have also found that they have rarely been provided a less than stellar appraisal or counseled on their behavior. Many leaders would rather allow them to do their own thing than counsel them on their attitude and performance. They feel it's easier not to argue with them. Supervisors are often intimidated by these employees and would rather avoid the confrontation that an effective counseling can provide.

CAUTION:
If you have team members that have been in their current position for a while and are not performing to standard, do your research before counseling them. Look to see what positions they have held, what training they have had, and what their last evaluations looked like.

It is not always the fault of the team member that he has never been properly trained or counseled. So before breaking out the "play nice or move on" speech make sure he has been given every opportunity to succeed. You may have to change the type of counseling based on your findings.

回 凹

H I N T :
Don't assume just because a person holds a position that he knows his job.

回 凹

If you discover the team member has had the proper training and has been counseled on his behavior and/or performance then the "play nice or move on speech" is more than appropriate. If you find that counseling, mentoring, and training are not working, do not hesitate to fire a team member. A team member with a poor attitude can potentially reduce the effectiveness, productivity, and morale of the rest of the team. Intelligence and aptitude cannot make up for a poor attitude. Cut your losses, your team will be better off in the end.

回 回

H I N T :
Document all of your counseling to ensure you have a historical record.

回 回

Summary

As you can see, there are many different ways to counsel your team. The key is to be consistent, know your counselee, and do not put it off. If you have done the other five steps counseling will come very easy to you. Don't make it more difficult than it is because ultimately effective counseling leads to effective teams.

回 回

H I N T :
Documentation from counseling can and should assist you in completing annual appraisals or evaluations. It's difficult to remember everything that a team member has done throughout the year but if you conduct effective counseling sessions the evaluations practically write themselves.

回 回

CAUTION:

Don't rush when completing evaluations. You should spend as much time on your team member's evaluations as you would want your supervisor to spend on yours. It's a direct reflection of them, take the time to do them justice.

CHAPTER 21:

A leader's power will only last as long as the position they hold. A leader's influence will leave a lasting impression. Consider how you want to influence your team and what lasting impression you want to leave with them.

~ **Lori A. Strode**, Author, Lead Like You Mean It! ~

回 囝

RETURN THE FAVOR

Step 6— Take Care of Your Investment

One of the proudest moments, as a leader, is when you realize that one of your team members, under your tutelage, is ready for the next step. She is ready to move to the next level of her professional career because she has proven to be successful in her current position. Unfortunately, that next level is not always on your team. There will be instances when your team member is ready to move on to the next challenge, and that may mean leaving your team. Do not hold them back from doing so!

I know that it is difficult to train, mentor, coach, and develop a team member only to see her go somewhere else, but it's the right thing to do. Throughout your relationship with your team member she has worked hard to meet your expectations. She has grown, learned, and developed into a trustworthy, competent, faithful team member. She did this not only for her own career but for you and the team; return the favor and support her efforts of continued growth and development. Let her go!

Don't wait for her to realize her value; you should be talking her up and planting the seed throughout the organization. Let others know that you have a team member that is ready, willing, and able to take on additional challenges and responsibilities. Inform your team member about job openings that are coming up. Talk to hiring officials about her skills and abilities. Help her prepare and edit her resume. Write letters of recommendation on her behalf to add to application packets. Mentor and coach her on positions that you believe would be a good fit. Set her up for success just as she did you.

Whatever you do, do not hold these team members back from opportunities that could enhance their careers and improve the organization.

Sure it will be difficult to replace a stellar employee, but if you have been preparing other team members along the way and telling them they are next, then they will be ready for the challenge. Healthy, planned turnover within the team is necessary for continued growth of the team and the team members. When you lose a key team member you gain so much more.

- Opportunities for others to excel
- Fresh ideas, solutions, and opinions
- New skill sets emerge
- Challenges the team to work together

When you are on the verge of losing a valued member of your team don't look at it as a loss, but rather another chapter of opportunities for other team members.

When a team member leaves, continue to provide support in the form of mentoring and coaching. Check up on him from time to time to make sure he is handling the new position. Make sure he knows that you are and will always be available if he needs assistance or guidance. He may not always ask for your help because he wants to prove he can do it on his own. A supportive email or a phone call is appropriate and generally appreciated. Your relationship doesn't have to end because the employment ended. Take care of your investment.

Ensure that each member of your team understands and lives by the *D.I.R.E.C.T* Approach. Understand that every person you touch, touches and impacts someone else. The *D.I.R.E.C.T* Approach is about compounding kindness, respect and humanity; one leader at a time. *D.I.R.E.C.T* your team, impact the future! Good Luck!

CHAPTER 22:

Talent wins games, but teamwork and
intelligence wins championships

~ **Michael Jordan**, NBA Hall of Famer ~

回 凹

IT WORKS

I have considered writing this book for some time. I wondered
if anyone would read it, and if they did, would they believe in
the process. Then, I asked myself two questions: Would I have
benefited from this book when I was younger or less experienced? Will people benefit from it now? The answer to both
questions was a resounding yes!

More importantly, I know the approach works, and
I believe in it. There are hundreds of different theories on leadership and team building, but this one is proven. It has been
proven with men and women, in war and in peace, and in aus-
tere environments and offices. It has been successful with
young and old, skilled and inexperienced, and bashful and
outgoing. I was able to write this book because of them, all of
them. Their words of encouragement and continued support
gave me the confidence to put this approach into words.

I decided that everyone has their own style, and maybe something in this book will resonate with you and assist you in being a better leader. Whether you are new to the role of leadership or a veteran, I hope you were able to take something away from the book that will prove useful for you and your team.

I pray for you to have the same success that I have been blessed with, but more than anything that this approach will lead to lifelong friendships for you and your team, similar to those that I have developed with mine. I enclosed a couple of pictures of two of my teams as a display of gratitude for their support, their professionalism, and their friendship. To all the teams that I have worked for and with, thank you!

= || =

Camp Phoenix, Kabul Afghanistan, 2008: You can make fun
anywhere! Christmas morning

Camp Phoenix, Kabul Afghanistan, 2009

634th Brigade Support Battalion Full Time Staff, 2007"

Camp Phoenix, Kabul Afghanistan, 2008: Supporting our
team member before the morale, welfare and recreation event

References

Carver, R.P., Johnson, R.L., & Friedman, H.L. (1970). Factor analysis of the ability to comprehend time-compressed speech. (Final report for the National Institute for Health). Washington, DC: American Institute for Research.

Farwell, Terry (n.d.). Visual, Auditory, Kinesthetic Learners. school.familyeducation.com. Retrieved January 28, 2013, from http://school.familyeducation.com/intelligence/teaching-methods/38519.html

QUICK ORDER FORM
Ideal for use by

Mid-level – Entry Level – Aspiring managers and supervisors.

Items for Educational Use
Educators, organizations and government agencies should take advantage of volume discounts for use in classes, training, and mentoring programs.

Volume Discounts	Number of Items
10%	2-10
20%	11-50
30% *plus free shipping*	51-100
40% *plus free shipping*	101+

To Order:
Go to our website at: www.northernazimuthcoaching.com
Join our newsletter and receive other information on speaking engagements, seminars and training events.

Sales tax: Sales tax will be added based on individual state rates

Shipping by air:
- U.S.: Assessed for first book and a reduced cost for each additional product.
- International: TBD. Pricing upon request

Learn more about Lori and her company,

Northern Azimuth Coaching, LLC,
by visiting her website.
www.northernazimuthcoaching.com

Join the mailing list and receive a free gift: "Top Ten Tips
for Achieving Work – Life Balance"

**In addition to coaching, Northern Azimuth Coaching
performs:**
- Training Workshops
- Empowerment and Wellness Retreats
- Speaking Engagements
- Webinars

Find us on the web or join us on Facebook
www.northernazimuthcoaching.com
www.facebook.com/NACoach

Contact us for additional information:
info@northernazimuthcoaching.com

NOTES

NOTES

NOTES

NOTES

NOTES

NOTES

NOTES

NOTES

NOTES